PRAISE FOR THE TIEBREAKER

"Gamification can unlock our potential as well as our passions. Reading Rebecca Gibboney's book The Tiebreaker helps us by giving us ideas to use in our schools to help educators level up their learning. It is clear, Rebecca is sharing her playbook with us. Additionally it is clear that she cares about her players. She gives us ideas, inspiration, and time to recommit to our own learning. Get ready to get off the bench and win the game with this book."

— MICHAEL MATERA, TEACHER AND AUTHOR OF
EXPLORE LIKE A PIRATE

"Quit taking the game so seriously and read 'The Tiebreaker.' Coach Becky shares her keys to success for instructional coaching and provides examples from her [court]work on how to engage educators in on-the-job professional learning."

— BROOKE BEITER, DIRECTOR OF EDUCATIONAL
PLANNING, FORMER INSTRUCTIONAL COACH

"This book is a true 'game changer' for anyone in the field of education. Gibboney's coaching is honest, actionable, and a whole lot of fun to read! Her framework, inspired by her years as a basketball player and coach, dives deep into how to get the best results from your coaching practice. The book reminds us that no matter where we start on the court, with the right plays, we can all improve our game."

— ALLISON KEEFE, ENGLISH TEACHER, #GAMIFYED

"Instructional coaches and educators will easily connect with Gibboney's laid back style and her personal journey. The art of gamification is not easy to master, yet she honestly shares her ups and downs to provide others with a clear path to success."

— VICTORIA KROUT, ENGLISH TEACHER, FORMER INSTRUCTIONAL COACH

THE TIEBREAKER

A SCOUTING REPORT ON BUILDING A CULTURE FOR GAMIFICATION IN PROFESSIONAL LEARNING

REBECCA GIBBONEY

Copyright © 2020 by Rebecca Gibboney
Published by EduMatch®
PO Box 150324, Alexandria, VA 22315
www.edumatchpublishing.com

All rights reserved. No portion of this book may be reproduced in any form without permission from the publisher, except as permitted by U.S. copyright law. For permissions contact sarah@edumatch.org.

These books are available at special discounts when purchased in quantities of 10 or more for use as premiums, promotions fundraising, and educational use. For inquiries and details, contact the publisher: sarah@edumatch.org.

ISBN:

THE LINEUP

Foreword ix
Coach's Notes xiii
The Tiebreaker xvii

Part I
Pre-Game Talk 1

Developing a Mindset 3

Part II
The Game Plan 15

Quarter 1: "The Kick-Off" 17
Quarter 2: "Thriving Through the Holidays" 19
Quarter 3: "In It for the Long Haul" 21
Quarter 4: "That's a Wrap" 23

Part III
Keys to Victory 29

Key to Victory 1 31
Key to Victory 2 41
Key to Victory 3 57
Key to Victory 4 75
Key to Victory 5 95

Part IV
Postgame Huddle 111

Dear Struggling Teacher,	115
A Coach's Confession	117
Overtime	119
Learn firsthand how to be THE TIEBREAKER!	121
Other "Coaches" to Follow	123
Game Notes	125
Endnotes	127
Other EduMatch Titles	128

To all of my Tiebreakers

Thank you for coaching me up all of these years. Thank you for putting in the extra hours. Most importantly, thank you for coaching me through my failures so I could reach success.

To The Pennsylvania Institute of Instructional Coaching (PIIC)
My game changed when I started developing into a PIIC instructional coach seven years ago. I walked into a conference completely unaware of what I was getting into, but I left convinced that instructional coaching had to be part of who I was.

PIIC coaching transformed my relationship with learning and leading in education. I built strong relationships with my colleagues through non-evaluative before, during and after meetings, and I focused my efforts on the four quadrants of the PIIC model: one-on-one and small group support, collecting and analyzing data, evidence-based literacy strategies, and reflective and non-evaluative practices.

It is because of my PIIC family that this book has become a reality. I cannot thank them enough for the support and encouragement. For more information about PIIC, visit www.tpiic.org.

FOREWORD

DR. CHARLES GREEVY

> Nothing great was ever achieved without enthusiasm.
>
> — BOBBY KNIGHT, HENRY DAVID THOREAU

As a former middle school English teacher and principal, I appreciate that the great American writer, Henry David Thoreau, included this thinking in his 1830s transcendentalist philosophies.

But who am I kidding...?

...As a child of the '80s and '90s, I totally love the fact that this quote is also attributed to another greater American philosopher—basketball coach Bobby Knight! I literally laughed out loud when I found this quote and saw that both Thoreau and Coach Knight were credited with saying this. Coach Knight took his lumps during his career and is probably remembered as temperamental, but he also did something right as a coach.

He had to. He had crazy success in what he did. His players were successful. His schools were successful. His teams were champions.

But why?

Look him up, and you'll see...: ENTHUSIASM.

Bobby Knight coached with enthusiasm. He bounced around on the sidelines, was loved by those around him, and had an evident passion for what he did. Coaching basketball players is not very different (as one may think) from coaching adults—and better yet, from coaching adult teachers.

My friend and instructional coach, Rebecca Gibboney, has taken her often over-the-top enthusiasm for teaching students, coaching teachers, and coaching basketball and has packaged it into her book—*Tiebreaker: A Scouting Report for Gamifying Professional Learning in Education*. Coach Gibboney's delivery in this resource is not always formal in structure, but her approach is genuine, crazy, and yes, enthusiastic—just like her.

For five years, I fielded crazy idea after crazy idea from Rebecca as her building principal. And I loved every minute of it. See, before I even moved into our middle school, I pulled "Becky" into my previous office and asked her to be one of my champions. I loved her ideas, her youth, her energy, and her coaching mindset.

"Becky's" classroom was non-traditional, just like her coaching. She found ways to turn crazy ideas into fun, engaging, and meaningful lessons; I knew that she could do that for our new building, too.

And I was right.

Her same classroom and on-court enthusiasm translated very well into her coaching mentality. Her crazy ideas turned into learning opportunities for her colleagues. Her ideas turned into dynamic game plans for our classrooms. And dynamic game plans eventually turned into solid games of learning for not only the students in the building but also the adults.

In this work by this top 1% educator, you will not only see her passion for her coaching on and off the court, but also the energetic and enthusiastic ways that she has helped to make learning meaningful and fun.

COACH'S NOTES

I lace up my coaching shoes. I slip on my high-heels.
I shriek with my coaching voice. I yell with my teacher's voice.
The ball bounces. The language whispers.
The whistle blows. The bell rings.

My heart is torn. Sipping coffee, I sit here fingers to my chin, while half of my heart tugs at my education world, the other half my basketball world.

My basketball relationship started when the only boy my father ever allowed me to date went by the name Spalding.[1] I would carry Spalding everywhere. I would read to Spalding and talk to Spalding. No matter the season, I could always depend on him. From the age of five to the age of twenty-two, Spalding pulled me through the buzzer-beaters of life and bounced me back from life's upsets. From elementary school to college, it was a love-hate relationship. There were days I wanted to swish

Spalding through the net and days I wanted to bank him off the backboard. Yet, I cannot thank Spalding enough for giving me one of the most meaningful lessons of life: *perseverance through the daily grind.*

Without Spalding, I never would have experienced 5:30 wake up calls. Without Spalding, I would not wear the scar above my left eye. I would not understand the true meaning of having a second family. Most importantly, I would not understand that feeling of *failing forward* one defeat after another. It is the blood, the sweat, and the tears that I fought for daily. It was a fight for the sport that stole my heart at a young age—basketball.

At the age of twenty-two, my love for Spalding had to sit the bench. My heart started to speak a new love language—Spanish. Whisking me off on new *aventuras* and opening my eyes to *oportunidades* that I never experienced before, I landed myself a job in front of hundreds of students as a Spanish teacher. Some days we spoke the same language, while other days, it still seemed like we were speaking a foreign language. There were ups and downs, just like in any relationship. Yet, like Spalding, this relationship taught me an irreplaceable life lesson—*showing up.*

Every day, I enter the unknown. While my students are the same, the oversized baggage they wear under their weary eyes always changes. While I might be the same *Señora,* I am always trying to engage my students' curiosities in innovative ways. While the white, bland scenery of a traditional classroom may look the same one hundred and eighty days throughout the year, the secrets they hide change minute by minute. The only constant I promise my students and colleagues is that I show up for them every day. I show up to ignite their learning. I show up to lend a listening ear. I show up simply because I might be the only one in their lives who *does* show up.

But, here's the *secreto* that my love language has taught me. Eventually, my students and colleagues will show up for me. It may not be tomorrow, it may not be a week from now, it may not be five years from now. Eventually, they will show up. In fact, some already have.

Some don't believe that there is love at first sight; that love can fade. Some believe that there is that one burning love; that one true soulmate. I beg to differ. I think that there can be many loves in a lifetime and that love grows with time. I'd like to think that both of my loves can collide. I mean, Spalding could speak Spanish, right?

While I still speak Spanish, our relationship has changed over the past five years. I wanted to share the language and spread the love. I am that peace-love-unicorns-rainbows kind of girl—that girl you probably run in the other direction from at first glance of her "8:00 a.m." smile from afar.

Yep, that's me!

So, I had this epiphany. Why not share my love with *everyone?* Spalding. Spanish. These two passions do not need to be siloed in my life—they can co-exist and bring happiness to my students, my colleagues, and...me. As a result, when my administrator sent out an email for anyone interested in "Instructional Coaching," I figured, *what do I have to lose?* Go big or go home. I mean, why not?

Fast-forward to where my love language and Spalding coexist. Over the years, my torn heart has been mended, one game after the *otro*. While I share the love with my colleagues as an Instructional Coach, I also educate my students using *español*, the same language that captured my young college-girl heart. As the assistant women's basketball coach at Lycoming College, I dust off Spalding so that my college athletes develop the same love for the sport. I have found a way to blend my *aventuras* as an educator and as an assistant basketball coach. I hustle through the daily grind, one win or loss after the other. As seconds dwindle on the shot clock, I want that ball in my hands for the win. I want that ball in my hands to show up for those that matter most—my students, my colleagues, my friends, my athletes, my family. I play under pressure for the love of the most challenging, yet rewarding game out there: the game of education.

Dear Coach,

I'm emailing you for help.

I've dreamt of being an educator, but lately, I have not been feeling that spark. Everyone tells me that, as a teacher, every day is different. Yet, to me, every day has been feeling the same.

My alarm clock rings. I go to work. I deal with the same student issues. I smile because that is what I'm supposed to do; but am I really smiling? I go home. I work out. I make dinner. I grade. I go to bed. My alarm clock rings...

Is this what it is going to be for the next thirty years of my life? Am I being the worst teacher ever? I know I should show up for my students, but if I'm being honest with myself—and you—I'm not.

I know I have it in me (the teaching thing), but where is it? I'm ready for my inner teacher to wake up. I'm ready for it to ignite, but I need something to change. Just something...

Sorry, I know I'm venting. Perhaps you are not the person to whom I should be venting. You did tell us to reach out anytime. So, here it is....

Can you help?

Sincerely,
    A Struggling Teacher

I

PRE-GAME TALK

DEVELOPING A MINDSET

For all my fellow educators out there, like me, who wear too many hats to count (*yes, you*), admit it...you are tired. I get it! You are not alone; but I am here to tell you there is a solution.

Unfortunately, it is not a solution that I can call a thirty-second timeout to fix, but one that *you* can fix. It all comes down to thinking outside the box and making it happen.

Be relentless. Be persistent. Be consistent.

Step 1:

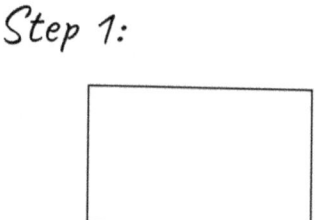

DO ME A FAVOR: draw a box in the air. Literally, do it. *Now!* Draw a box.

Place yourself in that box and think of the reality you are living in your job, in your building, or even in your classroom. Think about *your* reality. Not your dream classroom, not your neighboring teacher's classroom. *Your* classroom. *Your* school. Is it what you want it to be, or is now the time to change?

Step 2:

Are you having fun in your reality, or are you exhausted? Do you look forward to walking into your reality every day, or are you still cuddled under the blankets waiting for that next alarm to ring?

Now, glance outside the box. The area outside the box is what you really want for your reality. Perhaps you see a land of endless energy; or a land of colleagues that *pay it forward*, one smile after the next. Maybe your reality is asking a question and having a sea of hands eagerly raise to answer.

Perhaps you are imagining yourself going home to a healthy, warm dinner that you actually had time to prepare. Perhaps it is the extra time you spent taking your fur babies (yes, my dogs are my babies) on a long evening walk. Perhaps you envision a virtual field trip, robotic stations, authentic resources, etc.

Our teacher dreams are endless...but why can't our dreams become our realities? Who is stopping you? Administration? Students? Or are you stopping yourself?

Today, as you read this line, I am giving you my coaching challenge: classroom teacher, Instructional Coach, administrator (whatever role you might play)—*educate outside the box.*

You have an idea? DO IT! You have an epiphany? LIVE IT! You have a dream? GET IT!

6 | THE TIEBREAKER

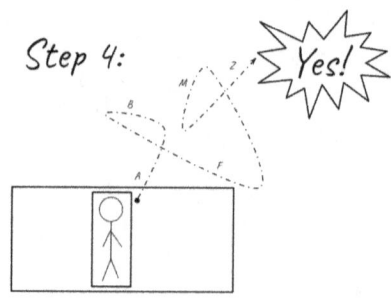

 Picture a line that is connecting where you are inside the box to your point outside the box. That is your ultimate goal—your journey. The journey usually is not a direct path. It is not a straight shot or an undefeated season. It includes twists, turns, bumps, and bruises. That is what makes it a journey: *your* journey.

 Develop a game plan (correction, *plans*) to get yourself there. You will need a plan A, plan B, plan C...plan Z. Whatever it takes! The journey might include strategies, coping mechanisms, perseverance, resilience, etc. There is no special play you can draw up for this journey, but from what I have found when there is a will, there is a way. Your game plan, your journey, takes many revisions to the drawing board and probably some extended time-outs. However, this journey, rooted in passion and values, will leave you victorious.

 So before you laugh at me and think, *Psh, Becky, this might work for you, but it's impossible for me*, I need you to travel back in time with me to my 25-year-old self. At this point in time, our school culture was at a standstill and something was missing. That flame? That spark? There was a hush in the crowd. A sigh of defeat. New coaches, new administrators. New teaching initiatives, new offensive plays. The score was lopsided.

That person that cuddled in the blankets every morning for that next alarm to sound—that was me! It took everything for me to get out of bed in the morning. That was my reality. That was me inside the box. My love language was slowly fading, and quite frankly, I felt lost. I did what every exhausted educator does. I shut my door, focused on what I needed to do between bells for my students, woke up the next day, and hit repeat. I barely interacted with colleagues; when I did, I smiled with a frown hidden deep inside. I became a teacher whom I never dreamt of becoming.

I lost touch with me.

I always envisioned myself, sleeves rolled up, interacting with my students. High heels just weren't in my personal dress code, because I was moving and grooving with my students every minute of class. For me, dress pants and Converse fit the part. I envisioned my door open, my classroom inviting. Most importantly, the smile I had written across my face was one that spoke truth and was contagious. That was my dream, and I needed to make that dream a reality once again.

It was time to come up with a new game plan (or game plans) before time expired.

Kevin Carroll, author of *Rules of the Red Rubber Ball*, challenged his readers to blur the line between work and play. As an educator, Instructional Coach, and college basketball coach, I accepted Kevin Carroll's challenge five years ago, alongside my administrator. I am happy to say we have never looked back. We took it upon ourselves to not only blend work and play but to make sure our colleagues accepted that same challenge. Is it easy? No. Is everyday fun? Absolutely not. However, it is our goal. It is what we strive for every day.

Instant Replay

Blending work and play is no easy feat. There no one size fits all, but that is the beauty of it. How you blend work and play starts with *you*.

Five years ago, we worked in a building where everything was strictly business. 7:45am the bell rang and teachers reported to their classrooms, followed by students. Teachers taught their eight periods every day and students listened. The dismissal bell rang and the students flooded the exits, followed by teachers with piles of 'teacher work' weighing them down.

Administrators would roll out initiative after initiative, mandate after mandate--John Collins Writing, Student Learning Objectives, Curriculum Alignment, technology, plus so much more.

We were hamsters spinning on a never-ending wheel. Some teachers kept spinning, holding on for dear life. Some stumbled off, never looking back again. While others only contributed to their daily exercise required each day.

Until, we added a little fun. The administrator and myself aligned building goals. We streamlined what we have in place and where we needed to go. We identified priorities and barriers. Then, we thought of solutions. What was the tiebreaker? The solutions were simply pure fun! Stay tuned...

Simon Sinek notes, "when the things you say and the things you do are in alignment with what you actually believe, a thriving culture emerges."

We needed to pack the stands again and bring back the winning culture instead of accepting mediocrity, a .500 season[1]. We needed to ignite the spark of our staff. We needed to bring the fun back into our building for our staff and students.

It was game time and, as the buzzer sounded, we had to make the call.

It was the tip-off into a new season—a season that blended gamification with professional development. As the clock expired and my heart beat faster, my two worlds collided: education and competition.

HUDDLE UP!

Alright, coach, listen up! Here's the thing: gamification and professional development is not something new. (I know that!) In fact, professional development has been around for ages, one initiative after another, one professional development after the next. It's like one sprint after another without a water break. Your teachers need that water break! For all of you statisticians and data analysts out there, here is the breakdown: professional development lasting 14 or fewer hours showed no positive and significant effects on learning. The largest effects were for programs offering more than 14 hours (Duncan et al., 2007).

30-second timeout.

Let that sink in. Breathe it in; breathe it out. Let me give you the play-by-play. If you give your teachers one professional development and then never revisit that content again, you have made no effect on learning. Yet, if you revisit this content multiple times throughout the year, you are making the biggest impact. Three-point swoosh! Slam dunk! The buzzer-beater victory!

Time-in.

Gamification, on the other hand, has been around just as long. Gamification, as Kapp (2014) defines it, is "using game-based mechanics, aesthetics and game thinking to engage people, motivate actions, promote learning, and solve problems" (p. 54). Growing up, it was the infamous family Monopoly© game that lasted hours or the intense version of classroom bingo with students nervously clinking chips on desks, waiting to shriek, "BINGO!" Nowadays, it's that fierce game of Jenga© or an engaging classroom battle of Kahoot©, where students have a dance move to each beat of Kahoot's theme song (or maybe that is just my students).

Coaching breakthrough: why not combine the two—gamification and professional development? Teachers are having fun throughout the year (yes, the whole year; not just the school year), re-visiting content delivered during professional development? In fact, don't even call it professional development anymore! Professional development is that one-stop-shop, that buzzer-beater you draw up to get the job done. This gamification of professional, ethical responsibility (initiatives, mandates, etc.) transforms professional development into professional learning.

Game-changer! #winning

I'm going to challenge you. You, the coach, the shot-caller, the catalyst, the leader: step outside of the box (remember that box?).

Step outside your comfort zone. What are you going to do in your building or classroom to pack the stands, to ignite that spark?

Take the leap.

If you are bored, your teachers are bored.

If your teachers are bored, your students are bored. Must I go on?

Let me be blunt, no one will ever want to join your team if you are not winners. Winners are not defined by state tests, nor are they defined by rigorous course offerings. Winners are defined by the smiles on students' faces and the high fives colleagues give each other when passing in the hallways. Winners are defined by the environment you create and the culture you foster.

So do your pre-game stretches, grab a glass of water, and put on those teacher glasses. It's time to study those keys to victory, develop your game plan, and celebrate with the world. What are you waiting for?

Can you play under pressure? Can you be the tiebreaker?

I challenge you!

Look in the mirror. What do you see? Similar to what Yul Brenner says as he coaches Junior Bevil in the movie *Cool Runnings* (1993), repeat after me:

I see passion.
I see a game-changer.
I see the *tiebreaker, who won't take defeat from nobody.*
The time is now.
Game on!

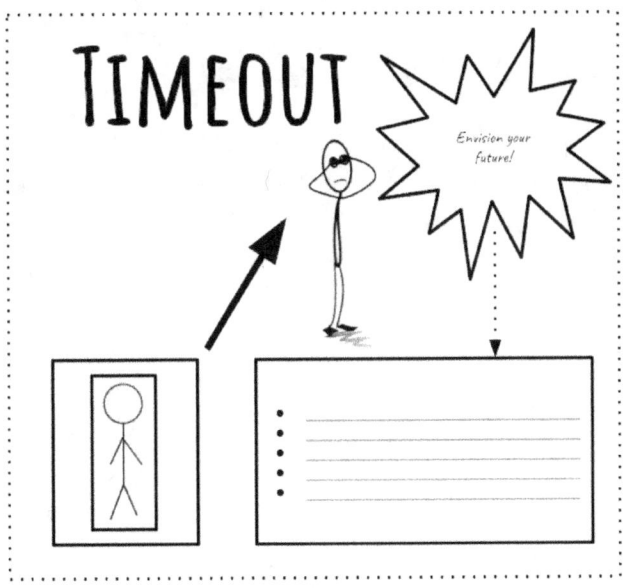

Timeout: Before continuing in this game, I need you to do one thing. Imagine that box again. Imagine what is outside the box. I want you to envision yourself outside that box. Take some time to write down (yes, write down) what you want for your future. Start with five. Then, narrow it to your top three. Finally, identify your top priority. Keep that image in your mind throughout this book. Focus on that priority. That will be your motivation. There are no excuses; there is only that image. It is your job to get yourself there. That will be your true victory.

II

THE GAME PLAN

Before jumping in, we need to make our game plan. I have always broken down the school year into four quarters (fitting, right?!). Depending on the quarter of the school year, there are different strengths and weaknesses of our teachers and our staff.

This section will break down the game plan quarter by quarter so gamification will best meet the needs of educators; and, to make it a three-point play, I have added some examples of my own gamification that I have tried with our staff at Loyalsock Township Middle School in Williamsport, Pennsylvania.

So, what are you waiting for?!

QUARTER 1: "THE KICK-OFF"

Approximately August–October

Strengths:

- Teachers are refreshed and rejuvenated
- Heavy time of year for professional learning
- Improve culture and climate right from day one
- Incorporate "getting to know you" challenges—especially for new teachers

Areas of Concern:

- Be careful not to overload teachers with "one more thing."

Possible Themes:

- Sports
- Halloween or fall
- Back to school
- Data review

QUARTER 2: "THRIVING THROUGH THE HOLIDAYS"

Approximately November—December

Strengths:

- Variety of themes to choose from
- Short, quick gamification chances
- Chance to revisit building-level initiatives
- Emphasize instruction, despite the holidays

Areas of Concern:

- Holidays make it difficult to hold longer challenges
- Keep it low-prep—teachers have many obligations

Possible Themes:**

- Thanksgiving
- Giving Thanks
- Christmas
- Kwanzaa
- Hanukkah
- Happy Holidays
- Sledding or dashing
- Building Your Snowman

**Some of the themes depend on the culture of your district.

QUARTER 3: "IN IT FOR THE LONG HAUL"

Approximately January—March

Strengths:

- Focus on teacher socio-emotional needs
- Not many holidays—makes a great chance for a longer challenge

Areas of Concern:

- Teachers tend to "hibernate" during this time of the year.
- Snow days (if you have them)—how will you account for these?

Possible Themes:

- Ringing in the New Year
- Valentine's Day
- St. Patrick's Day
- The 12 Days of Post-Holiday
- Dashing through the Snow

QUARTER 4: "THAT'S A WRAP"

Approximately April–June

Strengths:

- State testing is occurring (more than likely)—focus on some review
- Toward the end of the year, teachers have more time to reflect
- Help teachers wrap up their school year

Areas of Concern:

- State testing has many teachers concerned
- Teachers are just ready to finish the school year

Possible Themes:

- Review strategies
- Teacher reflection
- Student reflection strategies
- Spring

QUARTER 4: "THAT'S A WRAP"

LTMS Tailgate Challenge

Are you ready to kickoff another amazing school year?!

In order to kickoff another school year, we will be competing in our LTMS Tailgate Challenge. Like in the past, grade-level teams will be competing against one another (mini-course and related arts teachers will be assigned a team and special education teachers will be with their grade level).

Purpose:
- Build community within our building
- Understand Bloom's Taxonomy and Webb's DOK
- Integrate critical verbs and Collin's Writing into Bloom's and Webb's

How does it work?
- Certain points will be allocated to each team when a team member makes a "big play" (aka completes a task).
- Points will be updated once the 'big plays' are reviewed
- Winning team gets a surprise!

How do I accumulate points for my team?

QUARTER 4

<u>Fumble recovery – 1 point</u>
- Complete a Collin's Writing (any Type)
- Integrate a critical verb in a question stem
- Complete a low level DOK (1 or 2) or Bloom's (remember/understand)
- Take a 'team picture' with your best 'game face'.

<u>Safety – 2 points</u>
- Use a new app or website in your classroom.
- Write someone (a student or coworker) a pep talk and make their day. This should be thought provoking and meaningful! Show your proof by emailing me (rleid@loyalsocklancers.org) the note with a signature of the person who received your talk. *Extra point: act out the pep talk and really dramatize it! Send the proof (a recording) of your performance to me!*
- Complete a DOK (3 or 4) or Bloom's (Apply, analyze, evaluate, create)

<u>Field goal – 3 points</u>

- Share with a colleague an activity how you integrated all three (Webb's or Bloom's, critical verbs, and Collins) that <u>you tried out in your classroom.</u> Discuss if it was a success or something you need to adjust for future use. Email me evidence!
- Choose an area of focus and invite a colleague to visit your classroom to give you feedback.
- Email me 3 ways you connected or learned something new about your students in your Lancer Period.
- Give your Lancer Period a pep talk

Touchdown – 7 points
- Invite the coach to come in and check out critical thinking in action.
- Reflect with a coach about creating questions and create an activity or worksheet for the classroom using questioning strategies.
- Develop a low-level question and scaffold the question to eventually complete a high level question
- Create a lesson that encourages critical thinking in your classroom. Share with a co-worker and then make copies for your colleagues!
- Make team shirts for a dress down day. Everyone must wear them!

Interception – 7 points and deduct 3 points from any team
Complete a full BDA with a coach.

26 | QUARTER 4: "THAT'S A WRAP"

Tom the Turkey

Lost his feather over Thanksgiving! OH NO! Just like us teachers in our first week back, he's in a tizzy.

It's your job to help Tom the Turkey get his feathers back. How? Complete any of the following tasks by Friday and receive a a feather for each task.

Which team will help Tom get his feathers?!

1. Complete a John Collins Writing (Type 1, 2, 3, 4 OR 5) and show your coach student evidence.
2. Sign up to be a Pineapple classroom (see your coach for more details).
3. Complete an analysis activity in your classroom, using your team model and show your coach student evidence.
4. Share your favorite Thanksgiving memory, food OR tradition with someone OUTSIDE of your team and share it with your coach.
5. Tell someone in the building why you are thankful for them (be thoughtful) and share it with your coach.
6. Have your students annotate or close read a text and share student evidence with your coach.
7. Deconstruct a prompt! Got evidence? Show your coach the proof!
8. It's about those critical verbs! Share with your team how you taught a critical verb. Don't forget to share it with your coach for a feather!!!

Dress Tom the Turkey by Friday to win the prize!

Teacher Madness 2019
"Teacher Edition"
Who will advance and survive?
Team selection: March 11
Round 1 (for seeding): March 18-22
Final Four: March 25-29
Championship: April 1-5

Rules:
- Teachers will individually work to 'shoot' as many foul shots (+1 point task), pull-up jumpers (+2 point task) or three pointers (+3 point task).
- You may only complete each task once for each round.
- You must provide evidence for each 'shot'. Evidence can be provided in any form (text, email, mail, etc.)
- Points must be 'scored' (turned in) by Friday at 3:00pm each week to count for that round.

Game Plan:
3-pointers (3 points)
- Have students collect evidence to make an analysis.
- Invite a co-worker to see a lesson/strategy.
- Gamify one of your lessons.
- Students complete a Type 4 or Type 5 writing.
- Buy a cup of coffee, soda, or tea for a co-worker as a pick-me-up.
- Share a success from your day with a co-worker.
- Submit evidence of Level 4 DOK
- Create an innovative lesson!

Pull-up Jumpers (2 points)
- Thank 3 people throughout the day for something they did.
- Have your students complete a review strategy that you have found for your classroom.
- Students complete a Type 3 writing.
- Students work with the critical verbs.
- Collaborate with a co-worker.
- Incorporate a vocabulary strategy of choice.
- Students use a graphic organizer.
- Give a pep talk to a co-worker or student.
- Share 3 successes with a co-worker out of your team.
- Submit evidence of a Level 2 or 3 DOK

Foul shot (1 point)
- Students complete a Type 1 or Type 2 writing.
- Give 3 genuine compliments to a co-worker outside of your team.
- Students text render or annotate the text.
- Learn something new about a co-worker.
- Submit evidence of a Level 1 DOK

Overtime Points
FORCE A TURNOVER → STEAL 2 points from your opponent.
- Have a BDA with your instructional coach!

SCORE AN AND ONE → GET A JUMPER + A FREE THROW (3 POINTS TOTAL)
- Come up with your own 'shot' that has to deal with any instructional strategy and share it with your coach

III

KEYS TO VICTORY

Before every game, our coaching staff identifies three to five keys to victory for the upcoming game. They are our focus—our goals—for our players in order to excel in competition. Better yet, it is our way of preparing our athletes for success.

This section will do just that for you. Before diving in, take some time to digest these simple, yet important, keys to victory for gamification. In my experience, I have found these keys to victory to be crucial in planning and prepping myself and my colleagues for success.

It is easy to cut corners so you don't finish the sprint last. It is easy to turn the page after skimming the words so you finish just a little faster. Yet, like I say to my athletes, what are you doing for your team then?

Practice makes perfect. Practice the words on these pages into perfection. Take the timeouts to reset your coaching mentality. Focus on these keys to victory, and success will be only one basket away.

It won't be easy; but, coach, it will be worth it.

KEY TO VICTORY 1

INVEST AND VALUE ALL OF YOUR STAFF

> *It's the little details that are vital. Little things make big things happen."*
>
> — *JOHN WOODEN*

Think about a colleague you work alongside. Is it the teacher next door? The teacher down the hall? Think about the teacher in the "other building." Can you picture him or her? Is it the teacher whom you see leading every professional development, or is it that teacher who walks around the halls with the over-exaggerated smile? The teacher who shines from the morning bell to the afternoon bell? Or is it the teacher who will only leave the classroom to make photocopies? The one that scurries out the door right at the dismissal bell? The one who eats lunch behind closed doors? The one who goes unnoticed?

Let me guess: you are either laughing hysterically or smirking out of the corner of your mouth because you have a clear image in your head. (It's okay, you do not have to admit that I am right—it is way too early in the game to start admitting that.)

We all have these teachers. Whether you are from Pennsylvania (like yours truly), Alaska, California, or the tiny state of Delaware, you can imagine these teachers. Teachers enter into the classroom from all different backgrounds, colleges, areas of expertise, etc. Yet, there is one thing that we all have in common—we all have a story.

Do you ever wonder why that certain teacher sprints out the door at dismissal bell? Why that teacher eats alone behind closed doors? Does he have a phobia? Does she talk with a mouth full of food? And for goodness' sake, how does that teacher smile all day like that? How many shots of espresso does she put in her coffee in the morning?

You are the coach; these teachers are your players. Whether you are leading those real MVPs (most valuable players[1]), motivating the role players, or coaching those bench players, you must invest in every single one. No player can skip a lap; no one can hide behind closed doors; and absolutely no one can go unnoticed. As Phil Jackson states, "The strength of the team is each individual member. The strength of each member is the team."

THE REAL MVPS

Your real MVPs, your natural leaders, are the teachers who will run a full marathon when others might just jog a 5k. They are the teachers who dive headfirst into the deep end while the others are still treading water in the shallow end. You plant the seed, step back, and *voila* they are off and running. Easy, peasy, lemon squeezy. As an instructional leader, they are your coachable players. Invest in these MVPs, because they are your 20%. According to the Pareto Principle, which can be adapted to a leadership mindset, your top 20% can yield the most rewards (Dam, 2019). Their energy and smile are contagious. These are the teachers who the rest of your staff will gravitate toward. Give them the game plan, get them on board, and see where they run. After all, you know they are not going to walk, they are going full sprint! Catch them if you can! Fuel them, empower them, and coach them up. Your MVPs will lead you.

ROLE PLAYERS

The other day I passed a veteran teacher, sprinting to the copier between classes, out of breath.

I questioned her, "Mrs. Hall, is everything okay?"

She responded, panting, "No. I forgot to make these copies. Now I have 2 minutes until the next class is coming, and I still need to make them. The copier better be having a good day and not acting up like yesterday. Sorry, I need to run!"

Before I knew it, she was out of my sight and fighting in line for the copier.

To her, one more thing just seems like that extra thirty-second sprint at the end of a three-hour practice. It seems I-M-P-O-S-S-I-B-L-E. In fact, one more thing, and she just might be done with it all.

But...she can't be! She is a crucial part of my team and an

excellent teacher in the classroom. She knows her role, and plays it well. Without her, the team might fall into shambles. Yet, how could I give her one more thing when she is so frazzled by one set of class copies?

Those 60% of teachers, the role players, in your building know their role to a T. Their lesson plans are out of this world and their organization skills unheard of. Heck, I wish I was a student in their classroom. Role players excel at whatever they do. Yet, they are so meticulous that one more thing could halt them right before the finish line.

Enter the coach. Your role players are your players in whom you must invest the most! Build up these teachers within their roles. Give them a direction. Provide them with some extra support. In my past experiences, these role players are potential MVPs; they just don't see it...yet.

You can invest in bigger ways, like spending some extra time developing lessons with them, co-teaching alongside them, or even giving them future teacher leadership roles. Yet, with the role models, I have realized that even the small gestures count: offering to make their copies for them, buying them a coffee one morning, showing up for them. Because they will give you the greatest reward in the end. They will show up for you.

BENCH PLAYERS

So what if they leave right at the dismissal bell? All I know is that for my next half marathon, I'm training with this teacher! Man, the way they sprint out of that door, you can only wonder what their mile time is. But I wonder if they are really interested in a running partner?

These bench players are your toughest players to reach. One day they might show up for practice; the next day, they decide they would rather miss practice completely. They are inconsistent and unpredictable. You are on their time. It makes you question, as the coach, if they are truly invested in the team or just invested in themselves. They are lacking purpose and passion. Perhaps they are so far removed that they have forgotten what purpose feels like.

While this may be your bottom 20% (and theories may suggest ignoring this 20%), I'm going to pull the coaching card and agree to disagree. Like the Basque proverb, *"a thread usually breaks from where it's thinnest,"* a team is only as strong as its weakest player.

You may not need to invest all of your energy in your bench players, but you still must invest. Frustrating? Yes. Exhausting? Without a doubt. But rewarding. Coach them by building a genuine relationship, asking for constructive feedback, and valuing their voice.

Sometimes, as a coach, you don't have all the answers. The simplest answer might come from sitting in silence and lending a listening ear. So sit and listen. Your bench players could find themselves earning playing time. When these players find their purpose and reignite their passion, they will begin to learn and become the real MVPs. So lace up those running shoes!

REALITY CHECK: a school is not only made up of MVPs. Nor is a school comprised of solely role players or bench players. In most schools, there is a blend of MVPs, role players, and bench players. Each school has its own dynamic that defines that school; and that, right there, is the beauty of it all. Each one of these team members plays a crucial part in the team as a whole. Without bench players, no one would ever truly hear the truth. Without role players, people would just continue doing their job halfway, completely oblivious to the small details. Without MVPs, no one would have time to stop and breathe. It is the job of the coach to create the perfect starting lineup to take home a victory, because each one of these players is necessary.

The victory does not necessarily mean taking home the World Cup title or the Larry O'Brien NBA Championship trophy. It does not necessarily mean becoming an award-winning school or achieving a perfect score on the SATs. No. Sometimes the biggest victories are overcoming the smallest feats—a simple touchdown or a three-point play. It could be a struggling teacher asking for help or not having a failed substitute one day.

Coach, it is your job to pump up those MVPs while still keeping them inbounds. It is your job to get that teacher out of his or her classroom for more than just photocopies. It is your job to encourage that one teacher to spend some time running to their colleagues at the bell instead of the door. It is your job to get the team to play for you! The team needs to show up every day rejuvenated and ready to compete. The team needs to feel a purpose to fight day in and day out for you and their students. The team needs to have a leader to turn to when they are ten seconds from the finish line, exhausted. How are you going to get them to that finish line? You are going to invest in them—every single one of them, because your school, ultimately, will be united as one, no matter the role, no matter the purpose. Each person will stand united. No man or woman will be left standing alone.

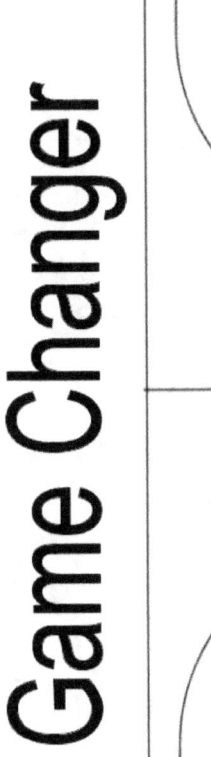
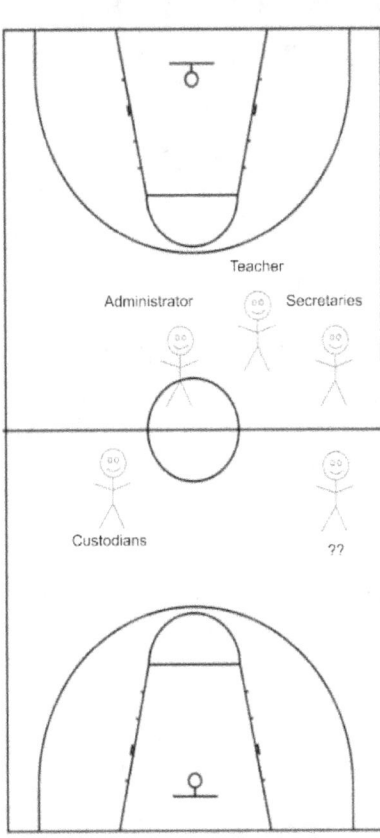

No matter the role, we all come to the center court, as co-creators, on the same team, ready to tipoff to a victory.

The question is, *how do you get everyone to center court?*

Really want to invest in all team players? Invite all players on board! Yes, that includes secretaries, custodians, paraprofessionals, etc. If they work in the school, find a way.

You don't always need to have a reason to show someone you care. Surprise someone at work once a week.

Timeout

Just like investing in your adult learners, investing in your students can be just as important. You, the coach; your students, the players. Each class brings its own team dynamic with all kinds of players. No matter if they are the MVPs, the role players or the bench players, they each deserve to have a coach that invests in each one of them. Think about your students. Who would be the real MVPs? The role players? The bench players? What can you do, as a coach, to get them to play for you?

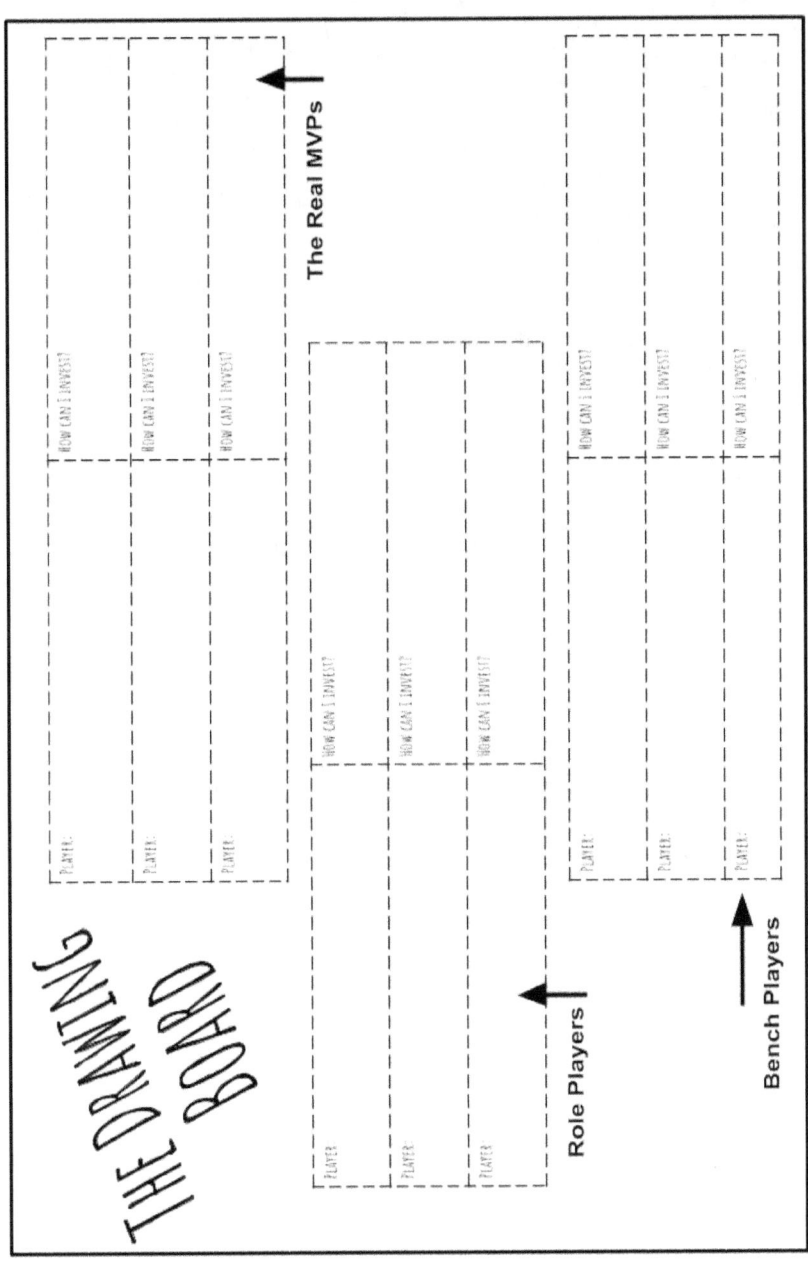

KEY TO VICTORY 2

DRIVING THE VISION

> *Champions are made from something they have deep inside them -- a desire, a dream, a vision."*
>
> — MUHAMMAD ALI

I have a confession—a true confession that took me about ten years to finally admit. Still, to this day, as I sit in the local coffee shop plugged into my Ellie Goulding playlist, my fingers are resisting the keyboard. Here it goes—I'm announcing it to the world.

I am attracted to the sparkly. I am attracted to the new and shiny. *Sigh.*

Full disclosure: I get my new coaching gear for the basketball season, and I wear it for a solid week straight. I may or may not wash it in between. (Shhh!) I get giddy, with that extra pep in my step, when light bulbs go off in my head about what I can implement in my classroom. No, not an idea for a month from now, or even a week from now. An idea I want to implement five minutes from now! Do not even get me started on my Amazon wish list...

So, let's just be upfront. I am that coworker who drinks that extra espresso shot each morning in her coffee.

My principal puts his phone on silent when I am at a conference, because he knows he will be receiving text after text. *Oh, we need to try this! How about if we did this?* In fact, I'm pretty sure he has a special ringtone to screen my calls on conference days. Now that I think about it, I am pretty sure the head coach of our basketball team might do the same as well.

Yes, I am attracted to the sparkle. Perhaps you are too? Or perhaps you are reading this and laughing because you have that pre-set ringtone for that special someone too?

Well, here I am, world. It's who I am and what drives me—the sparkle: the newest, most exciting "thing" out there (education or not).

Yet, one day the roles were reversed. I, the coach, received the coaching. After coming home from a three-day conference (and endless texts to my principal), my principal called me into his office to debrief. He looked at me, and I at him. All of a sudden, I did not feel like that giddy girl anymore with the extra pep in my step. *What was he going to say to me?*

"Beck, I really like your ideas, but I need you to slow down."

Slow down! I thought. Who has time to slow down? I'm not even sure if that's in my vocabulary.

"I don't want you to become so attracted to the shiny..." *Here it comes, wait for it...* "The sparkly."

There it was. I didn't know whether to run or hide.

The sparkly.

He completely called my bluff, but he was right.

Pause. Breath. Think.

My principal continued, "Beck, are you with me?" *Oh yes. Back to reality.* "I need us to slow down and think about our vision. I need us to align all of this back to our vision."

Lightbulb. Our vision. That's the buy-in!

Re-enter giddy girl. Re-enter the sparkle.

"Vision" is a funny word in education. Districts either have a vision, think they have a vision, or are so far off they do not even know where to start. A vision drives a sports team, an organization, a classroom, personal growth, and so much more. It is the coach's job to align everything to that vision.

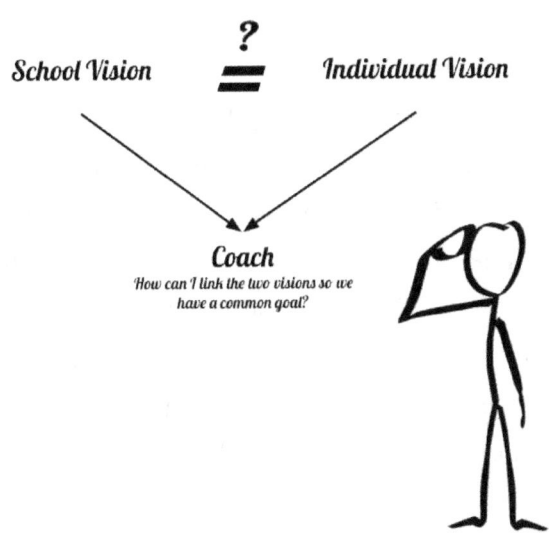

I, along with our women's basketball coaching staff, envision coaching winners. But we also strive to make improvements every day as coaches and student-athletes. We reinforce the importance of commitment, because without commitment, there is no improvement. Our players understand that we fight to produce competitive student-athletes in all aspects of the game, on and off the court. Our vision is their vision—it's a *shared* vision, and *that* is what makes the vision more powerful.

So what is the difference between the sports world and the education world? We all have visions, we all have goals—team goals and individual goals. Coach (yes, you), it is time to work smarter, not harder. Get your team on board and start shooting at the right basket under a shared vision.

If you are reading this book as a classroom teacher and have no idea what your vision is for your students or your own classroom, call a timeout, pick up a pencil, and start creating that vision.

If you are a leader and have no idea about your vision for your building or your district, pick up the phone and ask! Open those conversations, brew some coffee on a Saturday morning, and dive into some visionary work with teams of teachers.

Simon Sinek always says, "People don't buy what you do; they buy why you do it." Preach, Simon, preach! In our middle school building, Simon Sinek shifted our mindset in more ways than one. He challenged our team, from behind the computer screen and between book pages, to always lead with our why. Our "why" was our vision, and everything that fell under that had to support our vision. If a program or activity didn't fall under our "why," it was a no-go, and that program never saw any playing time.

30-second timeout: If you haven't heard of Simon Sinek (@SimonSinek), you need to get on his team, like, yesterday. Time in.

Three simple letters, one simple syllable: *Why?*

As a teacher, I always tell my students they have every right to ask why we are doing something. If I cannot answer the simple three-letter word for my students, then why am I making my students do it?

It is a simple question with a powerful answer.

TEAM VISION

The vision is your why. It is laying the foundation; it is your compelling purpose; it is your selling point. What that *why* looks like, from one team to another, one district to another, could be like apples to oranges. Each team, like each district, is different and has different needs. From winning a national championship to winning a conference championship ring, from giving every student a fair and equal education to helping each student achieve excellence, every vision is different—yet just as important as the rival team or neighboring district.

In my school, that looked like my administrative team developing what our building believed: *"Our goal is to provide students with experiences that will empower them to become thoughtful, meaningful contributors to society. Our teachers and staff are committed to offering students a wide range of learning experiences that will enable them to discover their passion and to discover how they learn best."*

INSTANT REPLAY

As we continued with our initiatives, my principal and myself always discussed what more we could do for our students and teachers. As we reviewed our vision year after year, we both felt that we were missing a community service piece that allowed our teachers to step outside of their comfort zone and facilitate time with students to develop them into contributing members of society.

We created, with the help from the teachers and staff as well, a period throughout the day called IMPACT. During this period our students were grouped, no matter their grade, based off of their interests. Each group was facilitated by teachers or staff with the intention to complete a community service opportunity that would impact themselves, the school community, local community or even the global community.

Year after year the program grew! It was astonishing to see how impactful it has become even today. We have had diversity cooking class, advisory council, and so much more! We even had a 5k. The beauty of it all...everything is facilitated and run by our students!

The power of a common vision. The power of coming together. The power of making an IMPACT!

As an instructional leader, educate yourself. Ask questions, and challenge beliefs. Make it uncomfortable. Discomfort leads to change. I, the coach, needed to believe in this vision as well. You have to buy in before you can get anyone else to buy in. That starts with you understanding the *why* of your administrative team. After all, I (like you) am the middleman between administration and teachers. You (yes, you!) are that MVP that can influence change and get the role players or bench players on board.

Once that vision is in place, use your coaching voice and let it be heard. Lead with your *why* and the team vision to recruit players to join your team! Educate your teachers. Educate your students. Educate your parents. Educate your community. You have the voice. Are you willing to use it?

TEAM GOALS

Once the vision is established, the team can start to establish some goals. Whether it be decreasing student tardy rates by 20% or increasing literacy scores by 30%, as the instructional leader, you must enter yourself in these conversations. You must set some long-term goals before game time. These goals will determine your team's success by the end of the season.

The administrative team at my school is required to create three building-level goals to report progress to the superintendent and school board once June rolls around. *Writing across all content areas, decrease failures, increase analysis, increase culture and morale, etc.*

Keep it simple, be intentional, and be realistic. Let's face it, too many goals and you will drive yourself crazy! If you have some goals already set, revisit them. Do your goals align with the shared vision? Can you measure them?

Most importantly, do your teachers know these goals? Remember, you are all on the same team. You are all fighting for that same vision!

If you don't have goals, don't sweat it! Take a deep breath, step back, and call a timeout. Pull your team together and go back to the drawing board. Without goals, where are you heading? How do you know you are on the right track?

Don't throw in the towel just yet. Instead, work harder. Blow your whistle. Huddle up with your team, not just at the start of the school year to share these goals, but throughout the year. Make some touchpoints, call some extra timeouts and regroup. Remember, the game of teaching isn't always a blowout win by 30 points, but more like a hard-fought battle in double overtime. A turnover does not mean the game is lost; it just means that you may need to call a timeout. Call a team meeting and open up conversations to share the successes and the struggles. Celebrate the good, the bad, and the ugly. Celebrate the twenty-point victories, the one-point losses, and even the twenty-point losses (not in your favor). Yes, even the ugly; because that ugly blowout is what is bringing your team one step closer to the next victory. You may not see it now, but you must believe. Believe in *your* team, believe in *your* goals, believe in *your why.*

INDIVIDUAL GOALS

Each basketball game, I have certain players that text me for individual goals. Some just need a look, some need verbal affirmation, and others just that written reminder. Either way, no matter if you are coaching MVPs, role players, or bench players, each teammate deserves to feel appreciated and the opportunity to grow within their role. It is your job, as a coach, to coach them up and help each team member determine their own potential. It is not your job to hold them back.

For me, that same mentality transfers to the education world. I have some teachers who need that positive morning text to get them moving, that thirty-minute lunch break, or even that social happy hour after work. I have teachers that need frequent check-ins, quarterly check-ins, or just the end-of-year check-ins. Whatever they need, I am their girl!

While it is important to direct the team as a whole, it's even more important to direct each member individually. Each teammate needs to feel heard, to feel appreciated, and to feel valued. They need to feel that sparkle when March comes around. They need to feel that extra push come May. Most importantly, they need to feel their worth when they step into their classroom every day.

How?

I know that sounds exhausting just reading it. I am one person, and my team consists of 30+ teachers.

So, how? Coaches are always taking care of others, but how do they take care of themselves?

The truth is that I am not the best person to ask when it comes to self-care. I am a work in progress. I could tell you to get a massage, a mani-pedi, go for a run, etc. Yet, the truth is, everyone has their own manner of self-care.

What fueled me was empowering my players. Sounds backward, right? Helping others helps me. So I encourage you to help your players create their own realistic, individual goals that align with the team goals. Help them monitor those goals, and get them back on track when they start to slip. Celebrate with them every small success, because individual success contributes to the team's success.

Hold them accountable so that they will hold the team accountable.

It is exhausting.

It is exhilarating.

It is rejuvenating.

Seeing my player successful after swerving off the tracks…seeing my player impact young lives with a smile after being on the verge of tears…hearing a teacher say, *I can do it*, when they left the day before defeated…those moments of success are my why. These are the reasons I coach. This is my sparkle.

ALL DECISIONS, whether behind classroom doors or on the basketball court, should be made with your team visions in mind. Our visions are what make our daily grind more purposeful and what drive young athletes to our programs. Our visions are the buy-in.

I am not talking about that vision that gets repeated verbatim on your in-service day or is plastered across district flyers. Sure, that is definitely a start; but I am challenging you to dig a little deeper. Ask your coworkers about the vision of the building. If they do not know, educate them. Brainstorm a list of activities, teaching practices, and programs that your building does, and categorize them under the vision. If the list does not align with the vision, I always question, *why then?* Is it just the sparkly?

Hard truth: your team is going nowhere without a vision.

The vision is the top of the ladder, but you cannot get to the top of the ladder without starting from the ground and lifting each other up rung by rung. Cheering each other on one individual goal at a time and working toward those team goals together are two ways to get to the top of the ladder victorious.

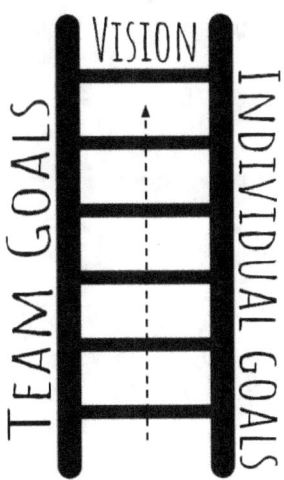

It takes time, it takes setbacks, and it takes redos. You are not always shining in the sparkle, because sometimes you are trudging through the mud.

Another hard truth: you are the coach, the leader, the visionary. Their success is your success; their failure is your failure. You have to own every up and every down. No one ever said that being a coach or leading would be easy, but it is 100% worth it.

Pause. Breathe. Reflect.

True confession: I am addicted to the sparkly, but I am not ashamed of that part of who I am. The sparkly is what keeps me driven, climbing up that ladder. The sparkly might get me off the vision track, but it also keeps me going.

Everyone needs a bit of sparkle. One deserves the excitement one gets with the first brew of coffee. That sparkle keeps you driven to work toward that individual goal, that team goal, and that *why*.

So what's your sparkle? What's your confession? Don't be afraid to share it. It could just be what you need to set you free and get you up that ladder.

Game Changer

- Find someone to hold yourself accountable. You cannot just hold everyone else accountable and forget about yourself.

    Accountability Teammate: _____

- Schedule some checkpoints. Open up your calendar now, yes now! Like...right now, and pencil them in! If not now, when?

    One week from now: _____

    One month from now: _____

    Three months from now: _____

    Six months from now: _____

    One year from now: _____

Timeout

Just like investing in your adult learners, investing in your students can be just as important. You, the coach; your students, the players. Each class brings its own team dynamic with all kinds of players. No matter if they are the MVPs, the role players or the bench players, they each deserve to have a coach that invests in each one of them. Think about your students. Who would be the real MVPs? The role players? The bench players? What can you do, as a coach, to get them to play for you?

THE DRAWING BOARD

Take that timeout, right now, to craft your vision. Whether a building administrator or teacher leader. Think about how what it is you want for whoever you are leading. Think about how it all aligns? If not, is there something that needs to change?

TEAM VISION:

TEAM GOALS:
(REMEMBER TO KEEP IT SHORT AND SWEET. THREE IS THE KEY!)

INDIVIDUAL GOALS:
(REMEMBER TO KEEP IT SHORT AND SWEET. THREE IS THE KEY!)

MY ROLE (HOW CAN I CONNECT ALL THREE TO CLIMB THE VISION LADDER?)

KEY TO VICTORY 3

RECRUIT YOUR DREAM TEAM

> *To me, teamwork is the beauty of our sport, where you have five acting as one. You become selfless."*
>
> — *MIKE KRZYZEWSKI*

In the game of basketball, there are five players from your team on the floor at one time. Those that start the game tend to be your five best players at that given time. To a spectator, these players are the "starting five": the best five athletes on the team. Which can be true. To some athletes, being part of the starting five can make or break a season.

Is that not true for educators? We have all felt the feeling of being left out, of pushed to the end of the bench, of being called last, or worse, forgotten when the building "coach" drafts their ideal committee from the lineup. That feeling of being last in a sprint to catch up to your deadlines.

Let's face it: we all like to be competing and on that playing field. But when you aren't part of that "starting five," the defeat begins to take over. You feel inadequate, you question your ability as an educator, and maybe you start job hunting in another school, another occupation. You work double-time, binge-eat, pour an extra glass of wine...you run yourself down.

Here I am, your coach, eye level with you. Sweat and tears in your eyes, I challenge you with the question, *for what?* We educators are just like the athletes. We are our own worst enemies, beating ourselves up over the small failures, talking ourselves out of those personal days because we just need to do one more thing, and labeling ourselves "bench players" if we aren't chosen for every committee our building administrator rolls out. We need to do one more thing to look better than our neighboring teacher and earn that spot on the dream team.

It is amazing how many athletes stray away from a sport they love or second-guess their abilities when they don't earn a starting spot. What will their peers think when they see them riding the bench? They have already worked so hard—how could they possibly work even harder?

So what do most do? They quit, because it is easier. Those that persevere are the elite and reap the benefits. They understand the true meaning of perseverance, resilience, and a relentless attitude. They understand that their time will come, because it always does—if not on the playing surface, then off the playing surface.

One constant with both kinds of players is the coach. The coach supports, plans, and motivates. No matter which athlete the coach is developing, it is his or her job to move these feelings of his or her players into action, united, as a team. Understand each teammate's strengths and weaknesses to guide the team toward victory.

Disclaimer: I am not advising against perfecting that starting five or pushing yourself toward excellence. Not at all! I am a victim of this myself. This is not a job where everyone gets a prize, nor should it be. The competition is healthy; wanting to be better, wanting to make that long-lasting impact, is daily motivation. What I am saying is to keep everything in perspective, because as a collegiate basketball coach, some things have recently become clearer to me. Things that I never understood as an athlete.

A starting five never needs to remain the same starting five for each game!

In the course of a basketball season, our starting lineup can change depending on our opponent. Consistency and team chemistry are important, but we often consider who we are playing. Is our opponent quicker than us? Taller than us? Do we match up correctly? How can we outplay our opponents to take home the victory? As a result, our "starting five" can change.

It does not mean one player is necessarily better than the other. It does not mean that the player will continue to start. Nor does it mean that the player is any less valuable than the rest of the team. It does mean that each player works harder every day to hold themselves accountable. It does mean that each person earns their playing time. It *does* mean that every person plays an integral part of the team.

Each day and each practice is even more important in preparing yourself and your team for that victory. So get out there, fine-tune your craft, learn your strength, and get to know your teammates. It is your job, coach, to make a dream team for whatever feat you aim to conquer. You have your players; now, you just need to find your dream team.

INSTANT REPLAY

As an instructional coach, I had many captains. In fact, for each of my initiatives or ideas (as crazy as they were) I wanted to implement, I first identified captains. Like I said, these were my colleagues who would reign me in, add a realistic perspective, and even challenged me.

For grade levels, it was the grade level team leader. For example, for our Student Learning Objectives (SLO), I always concurred with our team leaders with what was actually realistic for our teachers. For our text-dependent analysis initiative, I led with a committee of text-dependent analysis gurus! For our IMPACT project, I had a group of colleagues I always reflected with. For my classes, I had identified captains that provided effective feedback to me on a daily basis about my lessons.

I was surrounded by captains, good captains, that always pushed me to be a better educator and person in the game of education!

Who do you turn to in your classroom? With different initiatives?

THE CAPTAIN

Who is your first follower (Sivers, 2011)? When the ideas are stirring around in your head and you can barely find the edge of your seat, as you are bursting with excitement at the ideas formulating left and right, who is right there beside you feeding your fuel? And who is that person keeping you grounded in your seat, eagerly asking questions with excitement but still rooted in reality? This unique player is who you deem *captain*. This team player doesn't necessarily need to be an expert in the pedagogy, but this player brings the spark. His or her enthusiasm is contagious. You want the passion, the commitment, and the energy. Your captain is the one to bring it!

The relationship between the coach and the captain is one-of-a-kind. It is never perfect, and in fact, it is usually messy. However, the relationship is built off of mutual respect and honesty. While both individuals are knowledgeable, each brings a special quality to the playing field. As a coach, you are the driver and visionary. The captain is your first one on the floor every single day. The captain shoots the extra foul shots after practice. He or she goes that extra mile for you and his or her teammates, on and off the floor. Your captain is the role model, the marigold (Gozalez, 2013). The captain leads by example, always pushing his or her teammates to compete and to give his or her best no matter the circumstances. The Captain understands the shared vision and has a grasp on what the players are truly feeling.

You, coach, trust their opinion, value their beliefs, and respect them as an integral part of your team. You fuel, inspire, and empower them. When it is time to implement the new initiative or challenge, your captain becomes the implementer. You will find that, shortly after, many will follow. Why? Because everyone wants to be a winner. Your captain is a winner.

Instant Replay

I had colleagues that had some high aspirations for not only their students, but themselves.

One shooting guard, in particular, was an English Language Arts teacher. She worked tirelessly day in and day out. Some days she was on, and some days (even though I'm sure she was on) she felt she was off. She always put her kids first. Before school, during lunch, after school. Her room was a revolving door. It didn't matter how many tireless nights she had, she always got back up the next morning, a smile on her face, and answered her students' questions over and over again. She was relentless.

If I would approach her with an idea, no matter how out there it was, she always tried to understand. She would work after hours to implement. She practiced and practiced until she reached the goal.

This colleague turned out to be one of my best friends and mentors. To this day, I appreciate her work ethic and her 'in it to win it' mentality. Most importantly, I value her ability to fight for her students every single day!

SHOOTING GUARDS

For the eighteen years I played basketball, I don't think I would categorize myself as a solid shooter. I had my on-nights and my off-nights. When I was on, it was like no one could touch me—a shooting guard's dream. I could throw up the ugliest shot, and it would go in. When I was off, I was off. You know, those embarrassing moments where you completely airball, or worse yet, get stuffed by your own basket. Yep, guilty!

On those off-nights, I wanted to run and hide. I wanted to sub myself out and put myself behind the bench—not even on the bench, *behind* the bench. I mean, how could a college athlete get stuffed by her own basket? Well, guess what, it happens!

However, even on those poor shooting nights, my teammates would come up to me and give me a high five and tell me I'd make the next one. My coach would literally pull my chin up and tell me to keep shooting. My only choice was to keep shooting. I had no alternative. It was my role on my team. Shoot, shoot, and shoot some more. Wayne Gretzky encouraged shooters in ice hockey by saying, "you miss 100% of the shots you don't take." If I didn't shoot, if I didn't do what I was on the team to do, someone else would. Someone else would take my opportunity, my shot.

Technically speaking, in the game of basketball there are usually two shooting guards on the floor at a time. On *your* dream team, there are as many shooting guards as you wish. These shooting guards are relentless. They understand the importance of persistence, hit or miss. If they are "on," they are *on* and will keep shooting for that next challenge, that next goal, that next innovative strategy. Ask them how you can support them in their endeavor. Most importantly, let them keep shooting!

If they are "off," you might be that coach pacing the sidelines coaching them about shot selection. But you *must* keep believing in them. They might just need you to pull their chin up. It might take some early morning or late night workouts to keep them shooting. They will get there, because the more they shoot, the better the educator they will become.

The key to shooting guards is that they aim high. They have goals: a certain amount of points, a higher shooting percentage, increased student engagement, fewer student failures. Whatever it is, they have goals that push themselves forward to become better educators. They will shoot until they crush their goals, and then they will continue crushing goals one challenge at a time. It is in their blood; it is their competitive nature.

You need them on the floor, on your dream team, to achieve your team's goals. You set the goal, coach, and your shooting guards will be on the floor day in and day out working to meet it, despite the setbacks. Their job is to make it happen, one shot at a time. They are relentless. They are persistent. They are goal crushers. And they make it happen.

POWER FORWARD

On practice days when I was considered a power forward, I would internally jump for joy! That meant, during the fifteen-minute breakdown at practice between guards and forwards, I got to "rest." We practiced up and under moves, drop steps, and the mini-hook (which to this day, I still cannot do!). Meanwhile, the guards were running circles through shooting drills, defensive recovery drills, and one-on-one denial drills. Phew. I dodged that bullet.

Power forwards may not be the quickest or the most agile, but they are the most physical and willing to dive after loose balls. They are unafraid of a little contact and will not back down from their opponents. The team needs a rebound? Look to the power forward. The team needs a shot blocked? The power forward is on it. The team needs a putback around the rim? The "big girl"—the power forward—puts it in the hoop for two.

Perhaps it is fitting that they are referred to as the "big girls," because while typically they physically are the bigger and taller girls, they also have some of the biggest jobs to fill. They don't shy away from rolling up their sleeves and getting the job done for the team.

Your dream team is not complete without the power forwards. These are your go-to players that get the job done, no matter the time, effort, or commitment needed. They will roll up their sleeves to work side-by-side, clean up after your mess (I mean, no one's perfect, right?), and troubleshoot any issues that may come your way. They are your line of defense.

WITHOUT YOUR DREAM TEAM, you are a one-man team—alone and defenseless. It is your job, coach, to rally your supporters, create the buy-in, and give your supporters a reason to come into work every single day. This is different than your MVPs, role players, and bench players. While, yes, all players fall into these roles, only a few of these players will make the dream team.

In the average school year, there might be two or three initiatives that are rolled out. That's two or three initiatives that teachers roll their eyes, or quite frankly just ignore.

Why?

They are tired.

They are frustrated.

They are not supported.

So who usually takes on all the responsibility of initiative rollout? You, coach! You do! You are the initiative referee and the one making the bad calls. How can you play coach and referee? You can't, so don't even try.

You cannot possibly do it all alone. In fact, in my ten years of education, I have found it to be the opposite. You need as many players on your team as possible. If you want to make big changes, you need to think big. By thinking big, you need to build capacity. Here is the game plan: you create your dream team.

For me, I always asked for volunteers first. Always start with the willing! If there are no volunteers, you recruit. You play to people's strengths and help them see the payoff. As you continue to invest in all of your players, you start developing your dream team. Each initiative has its own dream team. There is no such thing as a single dream team, because each one of your players brings their own strengths to the floor. Pull them together now, coach!

Who are your leaders, your captains? Empower them. They will lead your initiative and rally up the cheerleaders to support your efforts.

Who are your goal-setters, your shooting guards? Keep them shooting. On the good days and bad days, they will shoot for only the best and keep your team fighting towards victory.

Who are your go-getters, your power forwards? Fall back on them. It's okay to show them your vulnerable side because they are here to listen and put you back on your two feet.

Your dream team will keep your initiatives fresh, keep teachers motivated about what they are doing in their classrooms, and provide a consistent educational dialogue for teachers and students.

Yet, as must any good coach, you must build the culture of leadership. Your players need to *want* to lead for you! Some believe that if you buy-in to them, they will buy-in to you and what you do. I cannot wave my magic wand or blow my whistle to make this happen. This takes practice. Every staff is different. It might take some frustration fights and some late nights.

As an educational leader, you are just like your employees. You are human, too! You all want what is best for those kiddos. You all have entered into the greatest occupation in hopes of changing the world—and what worked for me might not work for you. However, I have no doubt in my mind that you will draw something up. You will persevere, and you will be relentless.

Building capacity and educational leaders might seem tough, because it is...but it is the toughest moments that create champions.

> # TIMEOUT
>
> Let's take a thirty-second timeout and imagine the best leader you ever had in education, in college, or even in your personal life. What qualities did he or she possess? How did he or she make you feel? How did he or she leave you? List those qualities. Yes, physically write it down so that you can reference them! These qualities are now your game plan. These qualities are the same qualities you aspire to have as a leader.

Every coach needs their "person." Someone who is not just their captain, but rather a confidant. Instead of using the term *leader*, I prefer to use the bold word **mentor**. For years, my mentor made it clear that he was running alongside me. We were not better than the other, but rather each on the journey toward greatness together. My mentor always made me feel special by listening to my ideas (even the crazy ones). My mentor questioned me, even when it made me feel uncomfortable and frustrated. My mentor trusted me and picked me up when I fell. He took the blame when I took ten steps backward. My mentor was supportive. My mentor was challenging. My mentor was my sounding board. To this day, even though we are jobs apart, he continues to push me and inspire me. And that is the leader—correction: *mentor*—I aspire to be.

So, be that mentor who mentored you. Yet, bring your own coaching style, too. Coach your dream team with lessons from your past, abilities from your present, and goals for your future. Coach them up. Push them. Empower them. Your team will feel supported and inspired. They will run. They will fall. As long as you are by their side, they will always get back up for you. As long as you are always alongside them, they will do the most important thing of all in education...show up!

Game Changer

- Make sure each of your starting five teams feels valued. How might you do that? A simple thank you note, a fresh morning coffee, etc. Brainstorm below:

  _____
  _____
  _____
  _____
  _____
  _____
  _____
  _____
  _____
  _____

- While you might want to empower many colleagues, remember that sometimes when there are too many leaders it can get messy.

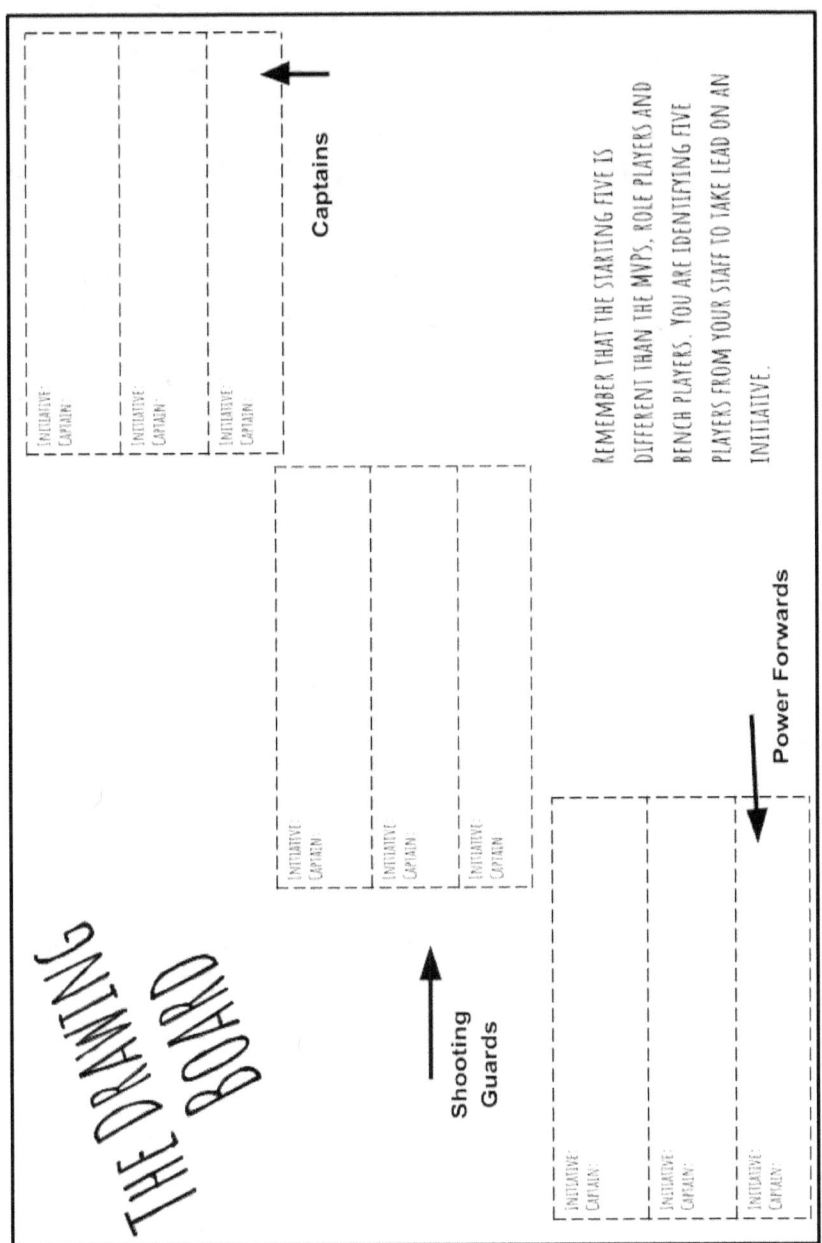

KEY TO VICTORY 4

LET'S TALK X'S AND O'S

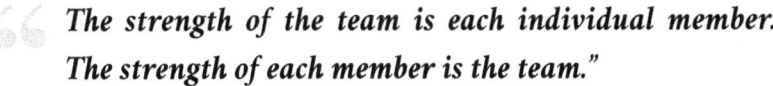

The strength of the team is each individual member. The strength of each member is the team."

— PHIL JACKSON

Entering my fifth year as an Instructional Coach at the middle school, I was ready for more. I spent the previous years transitioning into the role of Instructional Coach. I tried everything that one learns in Coaching 101. I built relationships, gained trust, provided resources, and so on. Within my first two years, I played with the idea of gamification for professional learning. I pitched a gamification challenge here and a challenge there. I will not say I was perfect in all aspects of coaching—heavens, no! I had teachers turn me away over and over again, disinterested in having someone visit their classroom. In some gamification challenges, I barely had anyone participate!

However, with practice and encouragement from my own dream team, I kept at it.

I was relentless. One crazy idea after the other. Some ideas were complete airballs, others slam dunks. Yet, from all of my trial and error, I started to gain some more confidence within myself to take on a more intense level of coaching.

In case you have not figured it out, I am *that* coach. On the sidelines, I am screaming at my players, spiking my high heels against the hardwood floors in attempts to get their attention between the chants of the crowd. In school, I am the Energizer Bunny© that continues beating the drum, even when the battery is running on low charge.

I always joke (but really in all seriousness) that I was (am) that girl that always says yes, dreams big, and works harder. The girl that never takes no for an answer. The powerful word *no* is just not in my vocabulary. Instead of "no," I hear "go." If game plan A doesn't get executed the right way, there is always game plan B, C, D, and so on. Like I said, I am relentless.

So, let me recap my crazy coaching side for you. Year one—getting my feet wet—my co-coach and I developed *Stall Wall* and hung newsletters in all of the teacher bathrooms. I mean, where else are you going to grab teachers' attention for longer than 30 seconds? Sadly, *Stall Wall* lasted only until the end of year one after a coworker told us it was a little creepy going to the bathroom with our faces staring at them. Touché. Point well taken.

Year two did not disappoint. My fellow Instructional Coaches and I proudly walked into our professional development session on the first day of school modeling matching baby blue tee shirts that read, "Keep Calm and Call an Instructional Coach." Yes, I went that far—guilty as charged. Better yet, my principal even wore one! I must also confess, I still continue to model that shirt today!

Year three and four followed suit. It was in these years that we were able to roll out our first mini-gamified professional development, and our teachers played along. We had finally created a culture through the intentionality of these Keys to Victory, plus morale-boosting activities like *Stall Wall*.

We started the school year with the low-risk scavenger hunts to refresh our staff on our initiatives. We surprised teachers with postcards in their mailboxes, gentle reminders that their Instructional Coach is always here! We blitzed them with magnets and lots of food to celebrate our successes! All these years I spent strategically making a game plan, taking into account the Xs and Os so that year five would top it all. I was ready for the next level, the championship.

- Maroon footballs with my contact information
- Welcome back baggies for classroom teachers and support staff
- Tailgate challenge planned, prepped, and ready to go

As I say, I was ready for so much more.

Year five also happened to be the year where we were going all-in with gamification. For every month, we had devised a theme. For every theme, there was some sort of gamification. Yes, you heard me. A challenge for each month of the school year. That's nine total, in case I just caught you counting the months on your fingers like me.

78 | THE TIEBREAKER

We kicked off with the *Tailgate Challenge* in September to jump-start the start of the new school year. *Boocabulary* for October. *Tom the Turkey* November. You get the gist. A lot of challenges, a lot of smiling, a lot of…coffee.

We knew it would take effort, preparation, and determination, but that did not matter. We saw results in the previous year, and teachers genuinely enjoyed making work fun. We were ready. The staff was ready. The game plan was set. What could possibly go wrong?

THE END of August rolled around, and teachers strolled into day one of professional development sun-kissed by summer, running on Dunkin'. (Sorry, Starbucks fans!) At our faculty meeting, we introduced our annual LTMS Tailgate Challenge. One by one, I tossed my maroon footballs out to the staff. Left and right through the air, touchdown passes and bobbled fumbles, until every teacher had my contact information. Point made. That was it. Loyalsock Township Middle School was ready to tackle the upcoming school year.

Week one, quarter one. Success with over 50% participation. My coaching schedule was filling up with before, during, and after classroom visits. Teachers were collaborating on lesson planning. Plus, teachers were eager to earn points and craving more!

Week two, quarter two. Not as successful, but we still had teachers participating. So I will chalk that up as a win.

Week three, quarter 3. A victory was starting to slip away. Less than half of the staff had participated in week 3, and my coaching hopes were quickly fading. My coffee cup, once half full, felt half empty.

Week four, quarter 4. We took the L. The energy and motivation of our staff had quickly disappeared, and the busy chaos of the daily teaching grind had taken over. So what did I do? I reached out to my dream team for their feedback as any good coach would.

"There is just so much going on. It was too long. I cannot keep track of everything I did in the week." The list went on.

Epic fail. I could hear the crowd chanting now, *airball, airball...*

It felt as if someone had passed me the ball when I wasn't looking and...*whack*...the ball hit me right in the face. If you have never experienced this, lucky you! It hurts, and it stings. I am not quite sure what pain is worse, the actual impact of the ball on your face, or the reality of the embarrassment you just experienced.

What was I to do? I had created a gamification challenge for each month! We had eight more challenges to go, and this was only the beginning. I could have stomped back to my bench, with each high heel digging into the wood floor. I could have thrown in the towel and hung up the whistle. I could have created excuse after excuse as to why the teachers did not complete the challenge—after all, they were to blame. How dare they! It's never the coach's fault. Right?

Ultimately, I could have given up. But that is just not me. Reminder, when game plan A fails, you turn to game plan B. Famous tennis player, Serena Williams's quote echoed in my head, "I really think a champion is defined not by their wins, but by how they can recover when they fall." How was I to recover?

Eventually, the sting wears off. The embarrassment becomes old news. The pain becomes your motivating factor, and your strength and resilience start to set in.

I took the rest of the day, or perhaps the week, to coach within my coaching box. I paced back and forth, no stomping necessary, reflecting on where *I* (not the teachers) had gone wrong. I re-evaluated my Xs and Os. I played back the tape. No, not my hugs and kisses, but the fine details of my original game plan. I did not throw in the towel or hang up the whistle, but rather, I ironed out a new game plan and faced the team with a new look and an even bigger smile.

The reality of it is that I was burning out my teachers, my key players, instead of empowering them to be the playmakers. I never believed the popular phrase, *less is more*, until now. Moreover, I had failed at the number one rule as a coach...listening. I needed to scale back, not just for the teachers, but for me, too. I needed to listen.

THE XS AND OS

In the sports world, we talk in Xs and Os. The Xs represent one team, and the Os represent the other. In this instance, my game plan didn't have the Xs versus the Os. Instead, my game plan consisted of both Xs and Os on the same team, working toward a victory together. Your Xs and Os are your playmakers. It is important to evaluate them for strengths and weaknesses. It is important to understand how one's weaknesses could be another's strengths. The players work together so that each and every one of them may shine during game time. They complement one another as they work toward a common goal, a victory.

So, in this case, sports enthusiasts, I'll need you to think outside of the coaching box and see how the Xs and Os in the education world play together on the same team to execute the perfect play. The Xs mark you, the coach, the leader. The Os represent your teachers, support staff, and employees.

THE XS - THE COACH, THE LEADER

Too often, we forget about ourselves. We tend to be people-pleasers, the caregivers, the make-everyone-happy-first kind of people. We are the MVPs, but sometimes the daily grind of doing everything perfectly becomes exhausting and buries us, mentally and physically.

It is okay to use a timeout. A 30-second timeout. A full timeout (one-minute).[1] A month timeout. Whatever kind of timeout you need.

It is okay to sip your coffee a little longer in the morning, breathing in the aroma of the fresh brew and savoring the warmth as it satisfies your morning wake-up call.

It is okay to put yourself first. Read that sentence again and look at yourself in the mirror. Yes! It is okay to put you first. It is not selfish. It is not irresponsible. It is necessary.

In fact, I am intentionally putting you first right now because what I have found throughout all of my coaching experiences, including more than just gamification, is that if I am not putting myself first, I cannot show up for my players when the buzzer sounds.

After four years of gamification, I have started to become deliberate about planning for myself first. Trust me when I say it is okay to think of your own schedule first. As a part-time coach and full-time teacher, did I honestly have the time to plan out gamifications for each month of the school year? Maybe. Did I have the time to collect, analyze, and have deep reflection with teachers each week about the practices and strategies they used throughout the week? Absolutely not. While I value ambition, creativity, and optimism, I had to come down off the clouds and be realistic. I had to blow away the sparkles and take a timeout. I had to listen to my body and my colleagues telling me, *NO*. It took until my first challenge in year five, the Tailgate Challenge, to realize it was just too much.

"Too much?" I always chuckle when people tell me I am doing too much. Deep down inside, I know they are right. (Shh, don't tell them that, though!) In all honesty, I cannot tell you what defines *too much* for you. Heck, I cannot even define that for myself. I normally don't know it's too much until I am barely treading water.

> **INSTANT REPLAY**
>
> For me, gamification was my way of fun. It was fun to come to work every day, but in reality, not everyone wanted to play the game. By listening and unpacking the film, I realized that I had to put my teachers first.
>
> We cut back on some of the gamification. We prioritized which initiatives would couple well with gamification. We listened to when our teachers needed some more fun.
>
> To us, it looked like a gamification a quarter. The basics and the goodies: Tailgate Challenge, March Madness, Luncheons and quick gamification blitzes.
>
> Keeping it simple. Bringing the fun.

You might be the coach that can conquer one gamification a month. You might be the coach that conquers one gamification a semester. A year. Whatever you can conquer, whatever you can fill your schedule with is great.

If I can share one important coaching tip, you need to be aware and truly honest with yourself. You need to figure out for yourself what is *too much*. You need to be okay admitting when you have had too much and when maybe you could add one more.

Let me clarify. As I mentor new educators coming into the "edusphere," I always hear that they are concerned with that *one more thing*. As a collective group, educators have put the fear (intentionally or not) into rookie educators that if they add one more thing, they will not be able to handle their main priority: the students.

Here comes my coaching rant.

Stop instilling fear!

We mustn't tell another person what they can and cannot put on their plate. Just because I can't handle a gamification each month of the year does not mean another coach couldn't. My primary goal for gamification was simply to have fun at work. It just so happened that when we started to see success, we decided to weave in some of our initiatives, and things took off.

To me, failure was inevitable. I did not expect everyone to participate. I expected some flops. I also expected some fun, and I knew I was willing to make some changes to make each gamification more successful.

My story, my life, is different from yours. One consistent, however, is a leader should encourage teachers to try. If they try one more thing and they succeed, high five them and yourself. You didn't hold them back! You empowered them. If they try and they get a basketball thrown in their face, high five them and yourself. Help them back up and teach them to move forward. They have now become more aware of what they can and cannot handle.

My hope in coaching is that my players *do*. They try and

succeed; they try and fail. I encourage them to stretch outside of their comfort zone—present at a professional conference, try flexible seating, apply for that grant, plus so much more. I believe in them. I walk alongside them, proving to them that they are not on this teaching journey alone. When they fail, I listen and empathize. I own their failure as my own. Just because this time may have been a failure does not mean that the next time will be. Either way, as their coach, I am there to cheer them on through success, and I am there to pull them up from defeat. So cheer on your players and lift them up. They will learn their *one more thing* on their own. I promise.

My mentor never let me flounder. While I may have gotten frustrated more than once with him, he always made me reflect as to why something may have failed or perhaps not succeeded in the way I had hoped. He is the one person that helped me become aware of my *one more thing*. We realized together through some failures that January and February are an awful time for me. *One more thing* could lead to ten more things. These two months are primetime for basketball. I simply cannot balance one more thing and do it well. Therefore, in our building, our gamification might be something short, simple, and straight to the point during these months.

Come September, March, or April, stay clear. We are in full game mode. Game faces are on! I know, I am aware that in those months I am ready to give my players my all!

Discovering your key role in the game plan is never easy. It could take a year. It could take five. Here's the secret, though. The beauty of life and leadership is that you are always discovering yourself. It is a process. In year five, I became aware of my *one more thing*. Yet, my self-discovery is not over. I will continue to become more aware of myself today, tomorrow, and even ten years from now.

So, my leaders and coaches, embrace your never-ending game toward self-discovery. You are the X. You are first and foremost. Each self-discovery is like a water break in training. You are quenching your thirst for leadership. While you trudge to a drink break, exhausted with sweat burning in your eyes, I can assure you that you will come out of that timeout fueled, stronger, and more determined than ever.

So, coach, take that extra sip of coffee. Take that extra deep breath. Take that rejuvenating water break. You deserve it.

THE O'S - THE COLLEAGUES

Your game plan isn't complete until you take care of the Os. The Os are the playmakers who will get the job done; the ones who will dive on that loose ball falling out of bounds; the ones who will put in that extra hour (or seven) to see their students succeed.

Remember, it is essential to invest in all of them: the MVPs, the role players, even the bench players. You cannot just fuel yourself and forget about the rest of your team. Keep in mind that gamification is meant to be fun and play, not one more thing on our teachers' plates. We want our teachers running into gamification ready to compete, fueled by excitement. We do not want our teachers strolling in late, grumbling under their breath about one more thing.

While being aware of your own limits can be difficult, it can be even more difficult to understand the limits of your players.

Some of your players will be easier to understand than others. Some might be guarded, others an open book. As educators, we value the importance of relationships as the fundamental building block toward. Your master game plan will never achieve anything if you do not take the time to build relationships with your Os.

Over the past nine years, I have found some strategies that have helped me form relationships with my Os. These strategies have allowed me to invest in all of my players. They are not mind-shattering strategies by any stretch. In fact, they are probably skills that we learn in our 100-level college courses. However, sometimes those simple ideas and reminders reinvent your own thinking. It is time that we reinvent your thinking—not the wheel.

THE COACH'S TOOLBOX

- Listen to Your Players with Intent

Intentionally get to know them. Listen to what is going on in their lives outside the classroom. Perhaps they work a second job. Maybe they go home to a family of six. What if they don't go home, because they hate being alone? Whatever their story is, get to know them cover-to-cover. It might mean sacrificing your lunch break or putting some grading aside, but the time you spend getting to know your colleagues is priceless.

These priceless moments support your colleagues more than you would ever imagine. Thirty seconds to lend an ear might be that pivotal moment in their day that shifts how the game is being played. During the past six months, I have been very purposeful when it comes to listening to others—not just colleagues, but even with family. I have truly tried to connect, make eye contact, and smile when listening to someone else.

Often, the person venting is not looking for advice or even a response. They are looking for a friend, a lending ear, an open heart. Find that purpose and set some intentions. You have it deep inside your open heart. Set aside that extra thirty seconds, because those thirty seconds could change the game.

- <u>Be Present</u>

As a leader, you wear many hats during the school day, not to mention the ten different hats in your collection at home. Teacher, counselor, parent, daughter, friend, coach—the list continues. Sooner or later, your hats start to fall off the hanger.

If you're like me, your mind goes a hundred miles a minute. You're smiling, you're breathing, you're listening. Yet, behind that smile, your mind is planning what you are making for dinner, what you are wearing tomorrow, and, hmmm…did you turn off your curling iron?

It is important that you, the coach, find a way to be present and focus on your players. Whether your player is behind a screen in an email or right in front of you, they deserve all of your attention. I will not lie, this is hard for me. It's almost as though listening and being present go hand-in-hand.

The fact of the matter is that distractions, daydreaming, whatever you prefer to call it, is natural. We are human; we are a work in progress. I catch myself wandering and attempt ("attempt" being the keyword) to redirect my focus (remember, work in progress).

You, me, and your coworker need to snap out of it. The leader in you needs to make it a priority to be present in every conversation. Mentally redirect yourself. Take a deep breath. Flip your phone over. Do whatever you can to stay present. Being present allows you to make your colleague feel valued and heard. Isn't that what everyone wants?

- Give and Take

THERE IS a famous proverb that *you can lead a horse to water, but you can't make them drink.* This proverb would play over and over in my mind to cope with the fact that not everyone wanted to play when it was game time. I would listen. I would bribe (just a little). I would engage. Not everyone would buy in.

I can remember being baffled that not everyone was *in it to win it*. I had to accept that not everyone wanted to be on my team, but it didn't stop me. Flashback: you are only as strong as your weakest link. Bench players were not the only ones lacking participation. I had MVPs sitting on the bench, too. Yet, the goal (for me) was to reach as many colleagues as I could.

So I listened.

I listened to what bogged them down. I listened to what kept them up at night. I listened to their frustrations, whatever they may have been. I simply listened.

I realized that if I wanted them to participate, I needed to lighten their load. If that meant running to make their copies as I was heading that way, I made their copies. If that meant covering their class when there was a failed substitute, I covered their class. If that meant picking up an extra coffee because I could see they needed an extra pick-me-up, Dunkin' Donuts© would be a morning stop before heading to school the next day.

I gave so they could take. I expected nothing in return. Would I have loved for them to participate? Sure! Did they? Not all of them. Relationships aren't built overnight. It takes months, years, decades to develop relationships. I've always been told that relationships are all about compromise—the give and take. It is not always easy. In fact, it is never really easy. Yet my players know that at any given moment, I have their back. And that, my friends, means more than anything to me.

One day, one practice, they will develop into a new player. They will bring a new game face, walk with a new confidence about them, and sweat through the uncomfortable situations. All it takes is a little give and take. The question is, how much are you willing to give?

- ## Practice Patience

IF THERE IS anything that I have learned from leading from the middle, it is that everyone learns and works at a different pace. Some run fast. Others jog in place. The walkers, well, they might just get lapped. We, as leaders, cannot assume that each of our players will grasp a concept at the same time in the same way.

Nor can we place judgment on a teammate or colleague if they get lapped or choose to jog in place. Eventually, they will finish the race at their own pace.

It is your job, coach, to practice patience, no matter how hard it might be for you. You must sprint alongside them. You must jog right next to them. You might have to watch as others lap you, just so long as your player is moving next to you in the right direction. And all of this you'll do with a smile.

My father is a very patient person. Me, not so much. He would always tell me, *Be patient, Rebecca. Patience is a virtue.* Being the typical teenager, I would always disregard and think to myself, *Sure, dad, whatever you say.*

It took me twenty years and leading from the middle to understand my father. No matter if you are working with students or adults, your patience is always being tested. There are times when you are ready to throw in the towel and forget the initiative altogether. There are times when you feel like you are so close, but then something happens, and you take ten steps backward.

Then, there are those times…those times when you wait it out. You persevere. You get lapped not once, but twice. Then it happens. You hit the game-winning jump shot; you finish the race. I've come to the realization that it doesn't matter if you are the sprinter or the person getting lapped. Each runner is just as important. The sprinter gets to the finish line. The jogger gets to that same finish line. As does the walker.

Practice patience with each player. Sprint, jog, walk, and enjoy the coaching journey, because I promise that you, too, will learn that *patience is a virtue.*

YEAR SIX WAS a breath of fresh air. I took off my leadership armor (Brené Brown, thank you for the reminder) and coached alongside my players completely vulnerable. Admitting one's faults, even in front of one person, is never easy. Try 30-plus. It never gets easier. It sucks, especially when you are the one who is supposed to be "leading the way." What I learned most from my mistakes is that it takes more of a leader to admit those faults than to continue to lead as though nothing ever happened.

Something did happen.

While I had all good intentions to help my colleagues, I overwhelmed them. While my game face was on, game mode in full swing, my players were running in the other direction, not looking back. While my fire was lit, their flame was dying.

All of my Xs were on the board, but my Os were missing. News flash: a game cannot carry on without its Xs or Os. The importance of having all players on the board cannot go unnoticed.

Take that water break. Take the cap off the marker and start drawing up your game plan (or game plans). Each time you mark an X or an O, remember they are important pieces in the plan. I have the privilege (yes, privilege) during basketball games to erase the board after each timeout. Don't be afraid to erase the game plan and start over. Starting over could be your biggest breakthrough yet.

Game Changer

Just like you do for your players, do for yourself. Open up your calendar and make a game plan. Each week, pick a specific day, a specific hour, for some self-care. Schedule it now, otherwise you'll find an excuse!

Day:
_____

Hour:
_____

Self-care:
_____
_____
_____
_____
_____
_____

THE DRAWING BOARD

THINK ABOUT THE COACHING TOOLBOX. WHAT DO YOU ALREADY DO FOR EACH COMPONENT AND COULD YOU DO MOVING FORWARD?

Coaching Tool	What I do currently	What I could do in the future
Listen to your players with intention		
Be present		
Practice patience		
Give and take		

KEY TO VICTORY 5

THE 'REGEN'

Definition: The act or process of regenerating or the state of being regenerated.

Forty minutes later and I've reached the point beyond exhaustion. My toes are bleeding through my socks from the continuous pounding against the hardwood floor. My knees aching, my arms bruised, my mind fatigued, pure exhaustion has set in for the price of victory.

My regen? A freezing cold ice bath to the point where your toes to your midsection go numb. (I cringe at the thought.) Yet, as an athlete, it was exactly what I needed to rejuvenate my old twenty-one year "athletic" body.

Did all of my teammates take ice baths? No. Did we stretch when the coach told us to? Of course not. As a basketball coach now, I do see the importance of regen work after a competition.

However, eleven years ago, my athletic self would laugh at the idea of regen.

Think about the power and importance of regenerating the body so that athletes can put forth max effort moving forward. Isn't that just like education? Isn't that just what our teachers need?

Ask yourself—when was the last time you practiced regen? When was the last time you rewarded yourself after a big "coaching" victory? When did you take the time to truly reflect on what went well in your day and what you could have improved? When did you persevere and try again, refining your work? If you can't think of a time, or perhaps it was just a month ago, get your coaching notebook out. Not for the Xs and Os, but for you, the coach, to practice the 'RE' Effect.

THE 'RE' EFFECT

> If you don't have time to do it right, when will you have time to do it over?"
>
> — JOHN WOODEN

The Act of REwarding

When I started basketball at a young age, I wore a shirt that read, "Go hard or go home." When I played basketball during my high school years, my assistant coach would always yell, "Go hard or go home." As a result, my life is carried out in one way. You guessed it: "Going hard."

Decorating my house, I go hard. Leading a healthy lifestyle, I go hard (okay, except for dark chocolate…you got me). Hosting a dinner party, I go hard. There is just no going home for me. For the past thirty-plus years, that was never an option, and for all of my colleagues, going hard is their only option. If you are going to do something, you might as well go 110%, right?

Needless to say, gamification with my colleagues did not fall short of this. Luckily, my principal liked to go hard, too!

By this point in our lives, we are all aware that there are two types of rewards and motivations: intrinsic and extrinsic. We also know that most people are motivated by extrinsic rewards. Now, I'm not saying that there aren't people out there that are purely intrinsically motivated. I'm sure a little thanks and appreciation can go a long way. The bragging rights are always a plus. That self-satisfaction of completing a task and checking it off the gameboard is just what you might need to sleep soundly at night. However, it is the 21st century, and most people want something for what they are doing. You just can't fight the truth.

When my principal and I were planning our gamification challenges for teachers, we knew that we were going to go hard (we had already established that). But what could we offer? It was time to think outside the box.

We sent out a survey to teachers. Their responses: more time, more money, a personal day, etc. Basically, the impossible. We knew that the rewards had to be compelling enough that our teachers would participate, but not **that** big (not saying we didn't try, though…).

Back to the drawing board. How could we meet some of their requests while not going THAT big? Technically speaking, we still had to receive approval from our superintendent for these rewards and meet teacher union regulations (Pennsylvania has teacher unions.) We could not bypass those two roadblocks.

One ridiculous idea after the next, we finally developed some pretty decent rewards to offer our teachers.

Thirty-second timeout.

TIMEOUT

You want to think about your challenges. If it's a smaller challenge that requires low-risk tasks, the rewards don't need to be as extreme. If you are planning a bigger challenge with some more high-risk tasks, you might want to think bigger.

Let me draw it out for you:

Low-risk challenges:
- Short challenges (one to two weeks)
- $5 gift cards
- raffle tickets for a prize basket
- small treats or coffee

High-risk challenges:
- Longer challenges (multiple months, semester-long, full year)
- Ice cream trucks
- Longer lunch breaks at Panera with Principal coverage (yes, you heard me)
- Dunkin delivery from our local radio announcer
- Marching band blitz

I had you at a longer lunch break, didn't I? Let me elaborate.

We knew we couldn't grant all of the teachers' wishes, but there had to be a way to meet them halfway. We got innovative. After taking in all considerations, we decided that we would treat the winners of our Tailgate Challenge to Panera© and—wait for it—an extra forty-five minutes to enjoy. No students running into the room while you're mid-bite. No need to rush to the bathroom. No interrupting phone calls. No emails buzzing through their computers. Just themselves, their team of teachers, and a nice, warm bowl of broccoli cheddar soup (my favorite!).

The day to reveal the winners arrived. The principal, assistant principal, and I rushed to award the winning 7th-grade team. They were shocked and could not believe what we were saying.

"Get going! What are you waiting for?" my principal urged.

"But what about our students during Extended Learning Time?"

"Get out of here. We have it covered."

That is all that the principal needed to say to reassure my colleagues. Smiles gleamed through their eyes, and one teacher was brought to tears.

"Thank you, thank you, thank you. This is exactly what I needed today," she reiterated. We later came to find out that her son was leaving town for an extended time that day. This extended lunch allowed her some time to visit and have lunch with him one last time.

We, as educators, can get caught up in the daily grading, the endless student needs, the overflowing work bags of lesson plans. Yet, if we don't stop to enjoy what we are doing, will we really reap the benefits? Will we see the beauty of our hard work? Will we rejuvenate ourselves enough to come in the next day fresh and with a clear focus?

Coach, it is your job to remind teachers to stop and reward themselves; and, yes, that might mean you rewarding them every so often for what they do every day. Sure, teachers will tell you they don't need anything for what they are doing. Don't listen to them. They need something. It could be a simple thank you, a freshly stocked gum drawer, or a longer lunch. Whatever it is, remember to reward your team after their hard-fought victory.

THE ACT of REflection

In any competition, there are two results: a victory or a loss. The result is black and white, never gray. While a coach always hopes for a victory, the loss is inevitable. There are going to be losses. No matter the result, win or loss, what should be consistent is the reflection.

Reflection is a critical part of the regen process. It lights the fuel. It teaches growth. It speaks the truth. In my basketball world, it looks like fifteen girls in the classroom, studying film, breaking down the positives and areas of improvement from the previous game. It is highlighting growth for each player. The beauty of game film (that players don't like) is that there is no hiding. You executed the play, or you didn't. You fouled, or you didn't. You face planted, or you didn't. In that case, we may rewatch in slow motion and laugh…with you, of course.

As educators, we probably fall victim to reflection more than the average person. We have committed ourselves to a life of learning, for good or bad. Some may view that as a negative. I tend to disagree. An educator dedicates their life to reflection. An educator fosters growth every single day. An educator embraces failure, because they realize that failure is the only way to propel themselves forward.

A coach leads by example. A coach enters different situations uniquely and intentionally. Coaches know where educators need to build stamina to go hard every day.

Altogether, they share, laugh, and learn from their failures. It is here that I use the word failure intentionally. In the previous chapter, I admitted my failures. They are not mistakes. They are not "oopsies." They are *failures*. As an educational society, we spend too much of our time in fear of admitting our failures, or worse, trying something new in fear of failing.

Well, coach, I am here to tell you and your team that you are going to lose. You are going to fail. I will also tell you that you are going to dust off the brush burns. You are going to wipe off the sweat. You might get a poor night's sleep, but you are going to face tomorrow like a champion and learn from your loss.

Not only will you grow from your losses, but also your victories. My basketball players are analyzing their play, not just following a loss, but also a victory. I am reflecting on my coaching technique after wins *and* losses. Why did something work here but not there? Why did we execute that play but not the other one that we practiced probably twenty times the day before? Why are my colleagues using this practice and not this one? How are our students receiving this newly-taught strategy?

The questions flood the coaching brain—good and bad.

So, how will *you* reflect with your team? That is the big question that only you can answer. No one size fits all. Reflection can be a touchy subject for individuals. Everyone loves to see what they do well but hide from what they do poorly. Do you blame them? It has taken me years to come to grips with admitting my weaknesses, being vulnerable. Yet, through it all, I have experienced the most professional and personal growth when showing up vulnerable.

You must first build a culture of reflection, which is never easy. I found the best way to do this was to model for my colleagues. I often reflected on my instructional coaching practices with my colleagues. I would identify what I thought was going well, but I also asked for feedback on ways we could have improved. I reflected on how I grew during a challenge and what I tried in my own classroom. I spoke the truth, and that was exactly what my colleagues appreciated.

I learned that I did not need to be an expert in anything and that I did not have all of the answers. People did not look to me to be 100% spot-on or some miracle worker. They hoped for the opposite. They wanted someone real.

That is exactly what I gave them—me. The non-evaluative and non-judgmental self embraced all of my colleagues' strengths and weaknesses. By being vulnerable, we were able to grow in a collaborative effort to build even more vulnerability, humility, and empathy. It was my goal to move each of them forward. It was my hope that they learned how to reflect on their classroom practices and strategies with me *and* be open enough to share with their colleagues.

As I continued to build this trust among myself and my colleagues, I started to think about how the process of reflection could be even more powerful. Sure, reflecting upon oneself is great—it's a start. Yet, we were a building working toward a common goal. How much more powerful could it have been if we reflected amongst each other?

So my principal and I went back to the drawing board.

Could we reflect after school? Nope. Who would stay for that? What about before school? I cannot even wake up before 7:00 a.m. Who would I be kidding? So, in reality, these built-in reflection times would have to be facilitated during the school day.

And just like that, it dawned on us! Voluntary reflection luncheons. After our big gamification challenges (The Tailgate Challenge, Teacher Madness, etc.), we held a themed reflection luncheon—the best part being that our cafeteria staff participated in the fun! Let me tell you, these were NACHO AVERAGE LUNCHEONS, with wildcat cheeseburgers for Teacher Madness and Alphabet Soup for vocabulary strategies, plus so much more. We went hard.

Teachers, secretaries, and paraprofessionals gathered with administrators and myself during their lunches to highlight different strategies they completed throughout gamification. We discussed what worked, what didn't, and how we knew our students had experienced success with our strategies. It was not "you did not do this," or "you did this." It was simply a sharing session.

These sharing sessions, what I like to refer to as "teacher talk," continued, eventually turning to not just luncheon discussions, but also grade-level team discussions. What we found was that by empowering our team leaders, they could facilitate these discussions with teams and lead to more productive, non-evaluative sessions of teacher talk. Wow! How powerful!

As an educator, the daily grind weighs me down. Somewhere in those hours between the early morning alarm clock (yes, 7:00 a.m. is early to me!) to the late-night grading, I squeeze in that teaching thing. Okay, so maybe it's not exactly like that, but some days *feel* like that.

Who am I kidding? It's a reality. We listen to professional development; we practice being present (to the best of our abilities); and we meet all of the state mandates. Yet, we are missing one huge piece in all of this: REFLECTION!

John Dewey states, "We do not learn from experience...we learn from reflecting on experience." Educators have thousands of different experiences every single day. They have, on average, twenty-five different experiences glaring back at them.

Look at your students. It is not only in our lessons where we can reflect and grow. That's only one facet. With each student interaction comes a new experience. Reflect on the teacher-student relationships you build and how you leave an everlasting impact on each one of them.

Without reflection, how can we grow? How can we learn? Coaches, it is crucial that somehow you find a way to build in teacher reflection. It can be informal "teacher talk" to serious meditation. Whatever you need to do. We urge our students to reflect daily. Perhaps we should listen to some of our own teaching.

Be the coach. Walk alongside your players through the reflection process, victories, and losses, so they leave school victorious. *And, pst...don't forget, you need to reflect along the way too.*

The Act of REfining

LOSING IS NEVER a fan-favorite for any team, but losing twice to the same team is definitely not an option.

So how do we, athletic coaches, prepare our teams for an opponent the second time around? We refine what we do. We go back to the drawing board, the Xs and Os. We break down the game film, capitalizing on our strengths while highlighting what didn't go so well the first time around.

As an educator, how do we prepare for the second time we try a lesson? Or how do we prepare for a student who is retaking a class? How do we prepare for the second semester? I'm hoping, as educators, we reflect and refine, but that may not always be the case.

If we do not reflect and refine, we will find ourselves back at square one. If you find a lesson successful, couldn't you always find a way to make it even better? If a lesson leaves you defeated, couldn't you make some adjustments for the next time around? The one thing you cannot do is just throw that lesson in the wastebasket and give up. No can do! It is time to learn from your reflections and refine your practices.

The act of refining could take many attempts. I am not saying that your lesson, your class, your gamification will be perfection the second time or even a third time. However, by refining the process each time, it will get better and better until you eventually leave that class or that school victorious.

When my Tailgate Challenge smacked me right in the face (airball), I reflected, and I gathered the data. I analyzed the numbers, and I listened to the feedback. For the upcoming year, I refined the challenge, and I couldn't have asked for a better result.

I only ran the challenge for a month, and the teachers had

basic challenges focused on the building-level goals and initiatives. Plus, I added some fun challenges just to shake 'em up a bit. The next year, the challenge got better, and again the following year.

When one refines something, one sometimes thinks it requires a drastic change. However, sometimes the smallest changes can make the biggest impact. Do not be afraid to refine a challenge once or twice, even three times, if that is what is needed. A good educational leader is always looking to refine, because, without refining, one would simply be complacent.

As a classroom teacher, I always felt that if I wasn't changing, I wasn't succeeding. In my opinion, there is no room for complacency in education.

This does not mean that you must flip everything year in and year out. Of course, there are times where what is working is working. I do believe that if it is not broken, do not fix it. However, there is always something we can improve for ourselves and for our students. An educator's job does not get any easier in year three or ten or twenty. Sure, the content might stay the same, and your lessons could stay the same—that is your choice. However, we live in an age where our world is changing fast, and knowledge is at our students' fingertips. If we do not change our lessons and curriculum to meet the needs of all of our students, are we really doing them justice?

In the same sense, as an educational leader, it is your job to throw in a buzzer-beater play or go for the slam dunk. No, I am not saying to always go for the sparkle. However, if you are still doing what you did thirty years ago and the data is not showing you successful results, perhaps it is time to reflect and refine. I challenge you to avoid being the leader that does the same professional development or the same expectations year after year. I challenge you to not fall into the same mold. I challenge you to be bold (thank you, @Wes_Kieschnick, #BoldSchool) and to change the game of education (thank you @MeehanEDU, #EDrenaline).

Most importantly, I challenge you to reward, reflect, and refine. Refine what you are doing until you like it. In fact, refine until it exceeds your expectations. After all, like John Wooden said, "If you don't have time to do it right, when will you have time to do it over?"

Game Changer

> Make sure that with all of these stages:
>
> **Reward**
> **Reflect**
> **Refine**
>
> you have some immediacy. Like with our students, the regen process cannot take place a month after the event. You must reward and reflect as soon as possible after a gamification in order to refine the practices for next time!

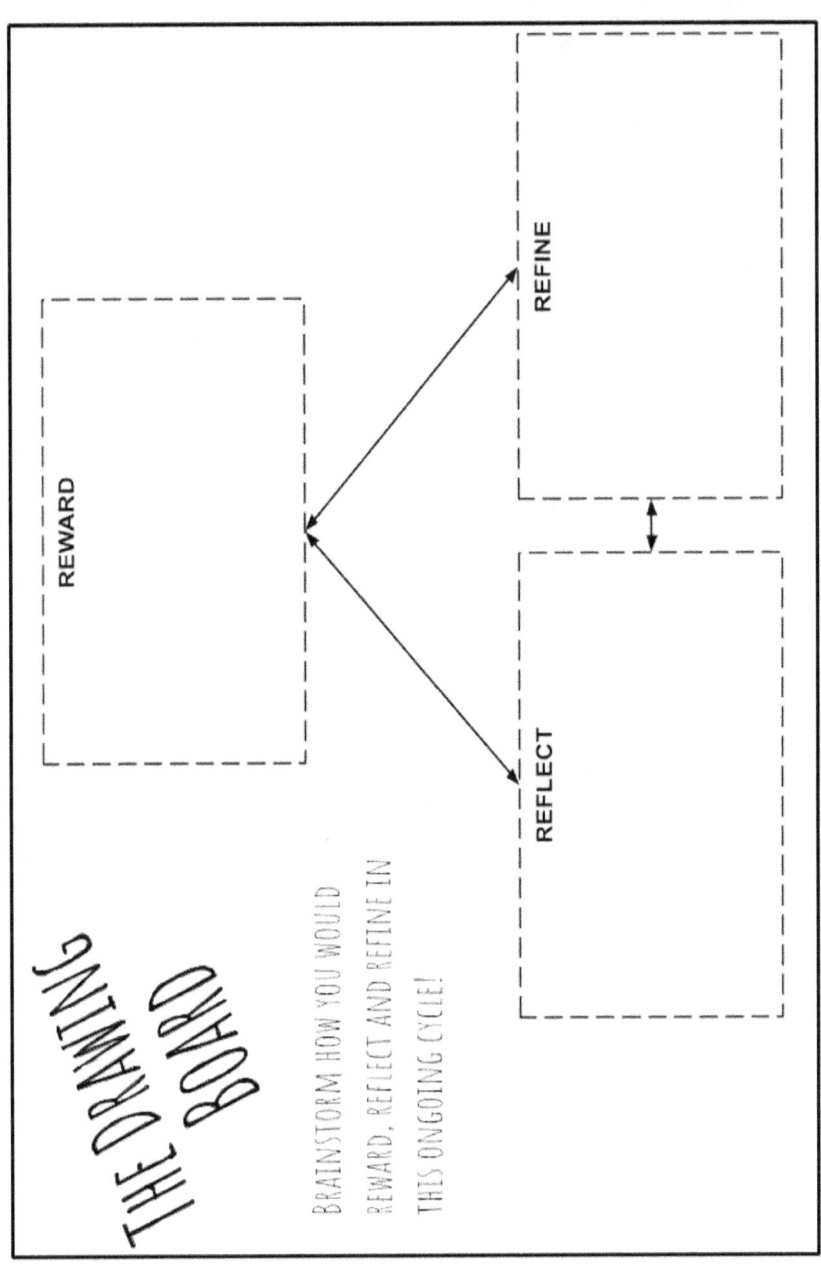

IV

POSTGAME HUDDLE

You win some, you lose some. You carry your head high, chin up, with confidence about yourself. You crumble; they all crumble.

It is all part of the game.

The over-achieving MVPs that get it sometimes faster than you. The role players that need you to run that extra mile alongside them. Yes, even those bench players that you might need to butter up to. Imagining that game plan A, B, C, and maybe even game plan Z. Leading the team with a vision, a drive, a passion.

It is all part of the game.

Recruiting your Os, your key players, to empowering your dream team. Understanding your role in the game. Empathizing with your players, coaching up their best efforts, and even their worst. Going back to the drawing board, day after day. Valuing that 'RE' effect: rewarding, reflecting, refining.

Coach, it is all part of the game.

If you want to leave your day victorious, it is the efforts outside of the playing court that count. As the coach, no one really has the chance to see what goes on behind the scenes, nor do they need to. However, those efforts are what differentiate a win from a loss. Like Steelers football coach, Mike Tomlin, states, "It's not what you are capable of; it's about what you are willing to do." Sure, anyone can show up to compete. Yet, not everyone has the endurance, the fundamentals, the keys to victory.

Before jumping right into the game plan, it is important to understand these five keys to victory and to start developing these practices within yourself, as a leader, as well as with your teachers, your players. It is important to value these keys and to make them come alive from the paper, to make these words jump from the pages.

How I see it, you have two game plans here:

GAME PLAN A: You can simply skim the words from the pages, close the book, and keep doing what you've always done.

Or…

GAME PLAN B: You can carry out the words from these pages and highlight your takeaways, post-its sticking out awkwardly from the book. You internalize these keys to victory so that in return, you create your own unique coaching style.

Whatever game plan you choose, carry this book as a reminder. The whistle is around your neck, the blank playbook turned over to you. New Xs, new Os. Coach, your dream team awaits.

The whistle dangles around my neck.

I memorize the stat line—10 rebounds, 3 student callouts, 4 reading strategies

I anxiously pace along the sideline, classroom to classroom.

The game isn't over.

The game has just begun

   Y recuerda...

   No soy el mejor en nada pero puedo mejorar en todo."

— RICKY RUBIO, NBA BASKETBALL PLAYER

Dear Struggling Teacher,

The ball is in your court now. Game on...

Sincerely,

Your Competitive Coach

A COACH'S CONFESSION

P.S.

Dear Reader,

*That struggling teacher was me, Rebecca Gibboney, in year five of teaching. It was, and still is, my **why** behind gamification. Yet, before I could get to the actual gamification, I had to build the culture (hence the reason for this book).*

It was then that I decided to be "The Tiebreaker." My husband always quotes Mike Tomlin, one of his favorite coaches, "The standard is...the standard." It took me a while to really let that sink in. There are no shortcuts, and there is no special treatment. The expectations are the expectations.

If something did not change, I would not have changed. My life (because, let's face it, my job is a huge part of my life) would have ended in a tie. I would have been living a life below standard. I could not let that happen.

I started to be intentional in my relationships with all staff and faculty. I questioned our vision and direction. I set goals. I found "my people" that inspired and motivated me--my starting five. I reflected. I had to be my own tiebreaker so that I could be my colleagues' tiebreaker.

I found that all of these keys are crucial, but one by far breaks the tie—reflection. Reflection is what shifts defeat to victory. We can sit in failure, be stagnant, and never move on, but where will that get us in education or in life? As a coach, and now more than ever, I have found the true importance of reflection. To be that tiebreaker for my colleagues, I needed them to understand and learn from their failures, so those defeats eventually became victories. I sat with them to reflect. I held luncheons to reflect in small groups. I encouraged reflective tasks through gamification.

The ball was in my court then. Now, it is in yours. What I did with my colleagues to build the culture towards gamification is unique. For you, it is a start, but the world is full of endless possibilities. I challenge you to make it your own! Share your successes...and your failures.

The score is 80–80.

Time has expired.

Overtime seconds away.

You are exhausted, and sweat is dripping. Marking period grades are due, and your coffee cup is empty.

Yet, there's something in you that's not letting you throw in the towel. Something that tugs at your heart. Something holding your smile in place. You are in this for a reason. Hold on to that something, and believe in that reason.

Be the Tiebreaker...

OVERTIME

Are you ready for more? Join the #tiebreakerEDU team! The game does not have to end just yet. You can be the tiebreaker!

The ultimate victory? It is my hope to build a FREE global hub comprised of adult gamification resources for all educators.

Just follow this simple game plan after you have read *The Tiebreaker* and attempted your first gamification with your staff:

1. Visit www.rebeccagibboney.com
2. Click on "Overtime" podcast and share your gamification challenge by completing the online form.
3. Rebecca Gibboney will be in touch with you to schedule a chance to share your experiences on the "Overtime" podcast and share your gamification resources (if interested).

It's time for us to all be on the same team and be the tiebreaker!

LEARN FIRSTHAND HOW TO BE THE TIEBREAKER!

Rebecca Gibboney can provide inspirational keynotes, workshops, professional development and consultations committed to instilling hope and fun for all educators. These presentations can also be customized to your event.

Her energy and passion will motivate participants to be *The Tiebreaker* and challenge educators to create a gamified atmosphere for educators. After all, gamification is not just for our students. Every adult is just a big kid at heart!

OTHER "COACHES" TO FOLLOW

Check out these amazing resources to bring gamification not just to adults, but to the students!

Edrenaline Rush - **John Meehan** - **@MeehanEDU** - **#EDrenaline**

Meehan, J. (2019). *EDrenaline Rush: Game-changing Student Engagement Inspired by Theme Parks, Mud Runs, and Escape Rooms.* Dave Burgess Consulting, Inc.

Explore Like a Pirate - **Michael Matera** - **@mrmatera** - **#XPLAP**

Matera, M. (2015). *Explore like a Pirate: Gamification and Game-Inspired Course Design to Engage, Enrich, and Elevate Your Learners.* Dave Burgess Consulting, Inc.

GAME NOTES

Duncan, T., Lee, S. W.-Y., Scarloss, B., Shapely, K., & Yoon, K. S. (2007). Reviewing the evidence on how teacher professional development affects student achievement. *Regional Educational Laboratory at Edvance Research, Inc., REL 2009* (033), (1-62). https://ies.ed.gov

Dam, R., F. (2019) *The Pareto Principle and How to be More Effective.* Interaction Design Foundation. https://www.interaction-design.org/

Gonzalez, J. (2013). *Find Your Marigold: The One Essential Rule for New Teachers.* Cult of Pedagogy. https://www.cultofpedagogy.com

Kapp, K. M., Blair, L., & Mesch, R. (2014). *The Gamification of Learning and Instruction Fieldbook.* San Francisco: Wiley.

Sivers, D. (2011). *First Follower: Leadership Lessons from a Dancing Guy* [Film]. https://sivers.org

ENDNOTES

COACH'S NOTES

1. Spalding - A brand of basketball gear and equipment. In this scenario, a basketball.

DEVELOPING A MINDSET

1. .500 season - when you have just as many wins as you do losses.

KEY TO VICTORY 1

1. Most valuable player - considered the best player on the team.

KEY TO VICTORY 4

1. In basketball, there are full timeouts and 30-second timeouts. Full timeouts last for one-minute.

OTHER EDUMATCH TITLES

EduMatch Snapshot in Education (2016)
In this collaborative project, twenty educators located throughout the United States share educational strategies that have worked well for them, both with students and in their professional practice.

The #EduMatch Teacher's Recipe Guide
Editors: Tammy Neil & Sarah Thomas
Dive in as fourteen international educators share their recipes for success, both literally and metaphorically!

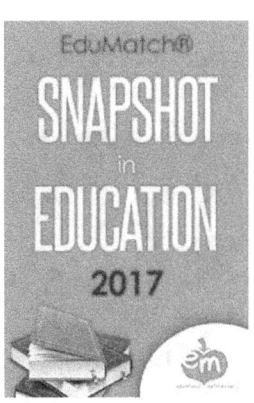

EduMatch Snapshot in Education (2017)
We're back! EduMatch proudly presents Snapshot in Education (2017). In this two-volume collection, 32 educators and one student share their tips for the classroom and professional practice.

OTHER EDUMATCH TITLES

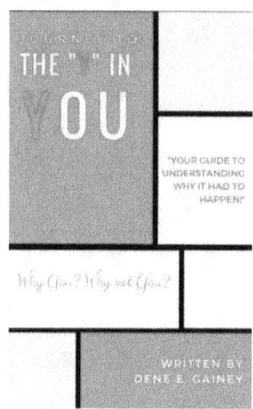

Journey to The "Y" in You by Dene Gainey
This book started as a series of separate writing pieces that were eventually woven together to form a fabric called The Y in You. The question is, "What's the 'why' in you?"

The Teacher's Journey by Brian Costello
Follow the Teacher's Journey with Brian as he weaves together the stories of seven incredible educators. Each step encourages educators at any level to reflect, grow, and connect.

OTHER EDUMATCH TITLES | 131

The Fire Within
Compiled and edited by Mandy Froehlich
Adversity itself is not what defines us. It is how we react to that adversity and the choices we make that creates who we are and how we will persevere.

EduMagic by Sam Fecich
This book challenges the thought that "teaching" begins only after certification and college graduation. Instead, it describes how students in teacher preparation programs have value to offer their future colleagues, even as they are learning to be teachers!

Makers in Schools
Editors: Susan Brown & Barbara Liedahl
The maker mindset sets the stage for the Fourth Industrial Revolution, empowering educators to guide their students.

Divergent EDU by Mandy Froehlich
The concept of being innovative can be made to sound so simple. But what if the development of the innovative thinking isn't the only roadblock?

EduMatch Snapshot in Education (2018)
EduMatch® is back for our third annual Snapshot in Education. Dive in as 21 educators share a snapshot of what they learned, what they did, and how they grew in 2018.

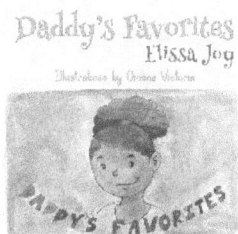

Daddy's Favorites by Elissa Joy
Illustrated by Dionne Victoria

Five-year-old Jill wants to be the center of everyone's world. But, her most favorite person in the world, without fail, is her Daddy. But Daddy has to be Daddy, and most times that means he has to be there when everyone needs him, especially when her brother Danny needs him.

134 | OTHER EDUMATCH TITLES

Level Up Leadership by Brian Kulak

Gaming has captivated its players for generations and cemented itself as a fundamental part of our culture. In order to reach the end of the game, they all need to level up.

DigCit Kids edited by Marialice Curran & Curran Dee

This book is a compilation of stories, starting with our own mother and son story, and shares examples from both parents and educators on how they embed digital citizenship at home and in the classroom.

Stories of EduInfluence by Brent Coley

In *Stories of EduInfluence*, veteran educator Brent Coley shares stories from more than two decades in the classroom and front office.

The Edupreneur by Dr. Will

The Edupreneur is a 2019 documentary film that takes you on a journey into the successes and challenges of some of the most recognized names in K-12 education consulting.

In Other Words by Rachelle Dene Poth

In Other Words is a book full of inspirational and thought-provoking quotes that have pushed the author's thinking and inspired her.

To Whom it May Concern
Editors: Sarah-Jane Thomas, PhD & Nicol R. Howard, PhD
In To Whom it May Concern..., you will read a collaboration between two Master's in Education classes at two universities on opposite coasts of the United States.

OTHER EDUMATCH TITLES | 137

One Drop of Kindness by Jeff Kubiak
This children's book, along with each of you, will change our world as we know it. It only takes One Drop of Kindness to fill a heart with love.

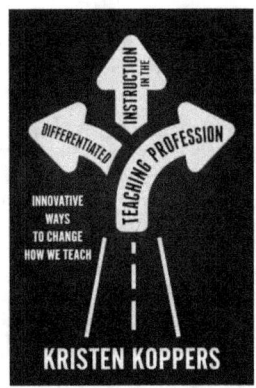

Differentiated Instruction in the Teaching Profession by Kristen Koppers
Differentiated Instruction in the Teaching Profession is an innovative way to use critical thinking skills to create strategies to help all students succeed. This book is for educators of all levels who want to take the next step into differentiating their instruction.

138 | OTHER EDUMATCH TITLES

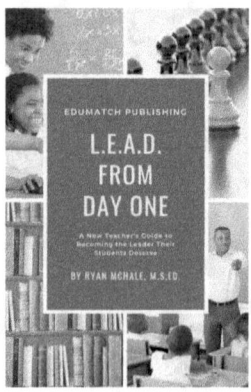

L.E.A.D. from Day One by Ryan McHale

L.E.A.D. from Day One is a go-to resource to help educators outline a future plan toward becoming a teacher leader. The purpose of this book is to help you see just how easily you can transform your entire mindset to become the leader your students need you to be.

Unlock Creativity by Jacie Maslyk

Every classroom is filled with creative potential. Unlock Creativity will help you discover opportunities that will make every student see themselves as a creative thinker.

Make Waves! by Hal Roberts

In Make Waves! Hal discusses 15 attributes of a great leader. He shares his varied experience as a teacher, leader, a player in the N.F.L., and a plethora of research to take you on a journey to emerge as leader of significance.

21 Lessons of Tech Integration Coaching by Martine Brown

In 21 Lessons of Tech Integration Coaching, Martine Brown provides a practical guide about how to use your skills to support and transform schools.

Everyone Can Learn Math by Alice Aspinall
How do you approach a math problem that challenges you? Do you keep trying until you reach a solution? Or are you like Amy, who gets frustrated easily and gives up?

EduMagic Shine On by Sam Fecich, Katy Gibson, Hannah Sansom, and Hannah Turk
EduMagic: A Guide for New Teachers picks up where EduMagic: A Guide for Preservice Teachers leaves off. Dr. Sam Fecich is back at the coffee shop and is now joined by three former students-turned-friends. She is excited to introduce you to these three young teachers: Katy Gibson, Hannah Sansom, and Hannah Turk.

OTHER EDUMATCH TITLES | 141

Unconventional by Rachelle Dene Poth

Unconventional will empower educators to take risks, explore new ideas and emerging technologies, and bring amazing changes to classrooms. Dive in to transform student learning and thrive in edu!

All In by Kristen Nan & Jacie Maslyk

Unlike Nevada's slogan of "what happens in Vegas, stays in Vegas," this book reminds us that what happens in the classroom, should never stay within the classroom!

142 | OTHER EDUMATCH TITLES

EduMatch Snapshot in Education 2019

EduMatch® is back for our fourth annual Snapshot in Education. Dive in as an international crew of educators share a snapshot of what they learned, what they did, and how they grew in 2019. Topics include Social Emotional Learning, identity, instructional tips, and much more!

Play? Yay! by BreAnn Fennell

Play? Yay! is a book my mom wrote for kids. I'm a toddler, and I like to read. I sit and look at pictures or point to my favorite pages. Do you like books like that? Then this book is for you too! The best part about this book is that you can read it with people like moms, dads, or grandparents. Get Play? Yay! today for fun, rhymes, and the gift of imagination.

OTHER EDUMATCH TITLES | 143

The EdCorps Classroom by Chris Aviles
In this how-to guide, Chris Aviles tells you how he accidentally stumbled into the world of student-run businesses, and how you can use them to provide authentic learning to your students.

Strive by Robert Dunlop
This book will get you thinking about how happy you are in your career and give you practical strategies to make changes that will truly impact your happiness.

Thinking About Teaching by Casey Jakubowski

This book explores the thoughts that author Casey T. Jakubowski, PhD has on a wide range of education related topics. Seeking to give voice to rural education, in this unstable time, and reflecting on a wide of research and experiences, this work offers all educators, from the beginning, all the way to the end, a reflective voice to channel their own experiences against and with on their journey.

I'm Sorry Story by Melody McAllister

Do you know what it's like to sit by yourself at lunch? Do you know how it feels when it seems everyone around you has close friends except you? That's exactly how Ryan feels. He wants good friends and he wants to be accepted by his classmates, but he isn't sure how to make that happen. Join him as he learns to put others first and make things right when he has been wrong!

OTHER EDUMATCH TITLES | 145

Define Your Why by Barbara Bray

Barbara Bray wrote Define Your WHY from the process she went through to figure out her WHY and through coaching others who did not feel valued, appreciated, or why they needed to live on purpose.

To the Edge by Kyle Anderson

From risks that resulted in immediate success to ones that elicited failure and regret, you surely will be inspired by Kyle's story. Take yourself to the edge and become more of a risk-taker in your life and career! #ToTheEdgeEDU

www.ingramcontent.com/pod-product-compliance
Lightning Source LLC
Chambersburg PA
CBHW071243070526
44583CB00017B/2306